INSTANT
ECONOMICS

For Isabel

THIS IS A WELBECK BOOK

First published in 2021 by Welbeck,
an imprint of Welbeck Non-Fiction Limited,
part of the Welbeck Publishing Group
20 Mortimer Street
London W1T 3JW

Design © Welbeck Non-Fiction Limited 2021
Text copyright © Welbeck Non-Fiction Limited 2021

A CIP catalogue for this book is available from the British Library.

ISBN 978-1-78739-419-3

Printed in Dubai

10 9 8 7 6 5 4 3 2 1

The images in this publication are reproduced from thenounproject.com with the exception of the
following pages 20 Heralder/Wikimedia Commons, 45 © economicsonline, 46 SilverStar via Wikimedia
Commons, 54 Public Domain, 57 Source TradingEconomics.com/Office of National Statistics, 59, 67 &
68 OpenStax College, 69 Bluemoose via Wikimedia Commons, 76 LDecola via Wikimedia Commons,
83 OECD (2020), 87 Cambridge Review of International Affairs, 90 William R. Shepherd, Historical
Atlas, New York, Henry Holt, 96 © Max Roser, 97 Data: Bureau of National Statistics, 103-105 Public
Domain,106 Economicshelp.org, 111 Public Domain, 124 Source TradingEconomics.com/Ministry
of Finance, Japan, 129 JLogan/Wikimedia Commons, 134 Corporate Finance Institute, 140 Public
Domain, 145 S & P Dow Jones Indices LLC, 147 Public Domain, 150 Wishnuyasa/Shutterstock, 153
Laurenrosenburger/Wikimedia Commons, 161 Credit Suisse Global Health Report, 162 Adapted from
Thomas Piketty's "Capital in the Twenty-first Century."

INSTANT
ECONOMICS

KEY THINKERS, THEORIES, CONCEPTS AND DEVELOPMENTS EXPLAINED ON A SINGLE PAGE

DAVID ORRELL

WELBECK

CONTENTS

BASICS

HISTORICAL OVERVIEW I

MICROECONOMICS

HISTORICAL OVERVIEW II

MACROECONOMICS

SYSTEMS AND INSTITUTIONS

MODELLING THE ECONOMY

MONEY

ECONOMIC GROWTH

FINANCE

MODELLING THE ECONOMY II

CHALLENGES

INTRODUCTION

This book is an introduction to the field of economics, presented in the form of 160 easily digested (but nutritious) topics, which cover both the long history of the subject – from ancient history to the present day – and its wide scope, from the market for gold to the market for complex financial derivatives.

Why is economics important, how has it affected the world, and why is it relevant for you? Until fairly recently, introductory books on economics could answer these questions, and motivate their readers, by summarizing a basic history, which typically went something like this:

Once upon a time, people used to exchange goods through barter. After a while they started using coins made of gold or silver, which made the market economy possible. For centuries, under systems such as feudalism, the size and scope of markets remained mostly small-scale, and our knowledge of economics was primitive. This changed in the eighteenth century as the Industrial Revolution powered economic growth, and economists beginning with Adam Smith argued that the "invisible hand" of the market drives prices to an equilibrium level, according to the law of supply and demand.

During the twentieth century, economists used sophisticated mathematical tools to scientifically prove that, just as Smith had predicted, free markets do lead to an optimal outcome, though subject to a number of caveats. It can even be claimed that, as one pundit put it, "The invisible hand gives you the iPhone."

Today, people working in finance use models developed by Nobel-winning economists to predict stock markets and manage risk to a high level of scientific precision, while policy-makers and the public rely on economists for an accurate understanding of complex social issues. The field of economics is a broad church that encompasses diverse approaches, but it supplies a generally consistent framework for understanding not just the economy, but many aspects of life, from happiness to how to manage the environment. Economics has never been more important than it is today.

Of course, we have now had time to absorb the lessons of the Great Financial Crisis (2007/8), so the above kind of narrative doesn't hold up so well. In fact, every sentence is at best only partly true (except for the last).

Money started with ancient credit systems, not coins. People have been thinking about economics since ancient times, and many of their teachings – such as the question of a "just price" – have been neglected by modern economists but are especially relevant today.

The "law of supply and demand" is not a law; there is no scientific proof of the invisible hand; engineers gave us the iPhone; prize-winning formulas came close to blowing up the economy; and there is a general sense that if economists can't predict a financial crisis, they probably aren't the best people to trust with preventing an environmental one.

Most importantly, economics is not an objective science, but a human pursuit where economic theories both reflect and shape the existing social context. Economic models can therefore be read as a kind of story about the world, which often say as much about the storyteller as they do about reality (and sometimes the old stories are the best).

This might be enough to put you off economics – but if anything it should do the opposite. Because economics really has never been more important than it is today.

The world is faced with a number of overlapping and interconnected problems, each of which involve economics, and whose solutions require new kinds of economic thinking.

One is inequality. As business leader and self-identified rich person Nick Hanauer warned his "fellow plutocrats" in a 2014 TED talk, "if wealth, power, and income continue to concentrate at the very tippy top, our society will change from a capitalist democracy to a neo-feudalist rentier society". If that is the case, we might soon be returning to the economic teachings of a thousand years ago for advice.

Another problem is financial instability. One lesson from the crisis was that existing economic models didn't just fail to predict the financial meltdown, they also helped cause it, by giving their users a false sense of security.

Finally, the climate crisis asks a question that traditional economics, with its emphasis on growth, seems fundamentally ill-equipped to answer – namely, are there limits to growth?

Fortunately, economics has historically made the most progress when faced with such crises. As we'll see, the Great Depression of the 1930s led to a new kind of economics, and the most recent crisis is having a similar effect, as economics looks to a range of fields from complexity science to biology in the search for new approaches.

This book will give an overview of economics that shows where conventional theory works, where it breaks down, and where alternative ideas are being used to address problems both old and new. The topics are divided into themes, and there is also a rough chronological order, but each is fairly self-contained so that readers can jump in anywhere.

The Nobel laureate radiochemist-turned-economist Frederick Soddy saw economics as occupying the space between matter and soul. As he wrote in his 1920 book *Cartesian Economics*: "It is in this middle field that economics lies, unaffected whether by the ultimate philosophy of the electron or the soul, and concerned rather with the interaction, with the middle world of life of these two end worlds of physics and mind in their commonest everyday aspects."

For a series of short glimpses into that mysterious world, read on.

WHAT IS ECONOMICS?

A traditional definition of economics is that economics is the science of scarcity.

ENDS AND MEANS

The English economist **Lionel Robbins** wrote in 1932 that "Economics is a **science which studies human behaviour** as a **relationship between ends and scarce means** which have **alternative uses**" and similar definitions still appear in modern textbooks. According to the *Economist* magazine, "The most concise, non-abusive, definition is **the study of how society uses its scarce resources**."

THE DISMAL SCIENCE

The nineteenth-century Victorian historian **Thomas Carlyle** famously called economics the "**dismal science**" (in an **article defending slavery**) and the emphasis on **scarcity** is one reason the label stuck.

THE SCIENCE OF MONEY

A simpler definition, which would apply to this book, is that economics is **the study of transactions involving money**.

As we'll see, economics exists at the **contested border** between the **sciences** and the **humanities**, and **combines** a **range of disciplines**, including **psychology**, **sociology**, **accounting**, **applied mathematics**, and so on.

Perhaps an easier question to ask is, **what does an economist do?**

But some see economics as a **method for analysing human systems in general**. The economist **Gary Becker** echoed **Robbins** when he wrote that "Economics is **the study of the allocation of scarce resources to satisfy competing ends**", but more generally he described the approach in 1976 as a **combination** of "**maximizing behaviour**, **stable preferences**, and **market equilibrium**, used **relentlessly** and **unflinchingly**".

WHAT DOES AN ECONOMIST DO?

Economists analyse data, research trends, and evaluate economic issues. They may work for academia, businesses, governments, think-tanks, banks, and so on. They are also invited on news shows to try to explain the crisis that just happened.

AN ECONOMIST'S LIFE

Economists are well paid. In 2018, the **median pay** for an **economist in the US** was $104,340. That compares with $78,650 for **social scientists** in general, or $38,640 for all occupations.

As we will see, economists may **specialize** in a number of different areas, including:

- **Microeconomics**: the behaviour of **individuals** and **firms**.

- **Macroeconomics**: big-picture things like **growth**, **unemployment**, and **inflation**.

- **Econometrics**: searching for **correlations** or **trends** in the **data**.

- **Finance**: **investments, markets, risk**.

- **Industrial organization**: the **structure** of **firms** and **markets**.

- **International economics**: **international trade**, the impact of **globalization**.

- **Labour economics**: **employment** and **wages**.

- **Public finance**: **government policies** on **tax**, **budgets**, etc.

THE MASTER-ECONOMIST

As the English economist **John Maynard Keynes** wrote in 1924, "the master-economist must possess a **rare combination of gifts**. He must be **mathematician, historian, statesman, philosopher** – in some degree. He must **understand symbols** and **speak in words**. He must contemplate the **particular** in terms of the **general** and touch **abstract** and **concrete** in the same **flight of thought**. He must study the **present** in the light of the **past** for the purposes of the **future**. No part of man's nature or his institutions must lie entirely outside his regard." No wonder they are well paid!

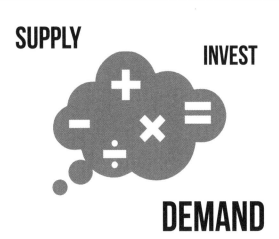

SUPPLY

INVEST

DEMAND

WHAT IS WEALTH?

A basic question in economics is how to improve wealth – which presumes we know what that is.

MATERIAL WEALTH

One **measure of wealth** is our **material well-being**, which overall has seen **enormous improvements**, especially over the last three hundred years since the **Industrial Revolution** kicked off.

We have also seen a **massive rise** in **other measures of prosperity**: we now **own more stuff**, and **more sophisticated toys and machines**, than at any time in history.

In the early nineteenth century, **life expectancy** in England was about forty years (in part because of **infant mortality**). It is now about **twice that**.

VIRTUAL WEALTH

Economics also deals with another kind of wealth that is rather different, namely **virtual wealth**. This has more to do with the **power to make something valuable through property rights**. For example, **Bill Gates** became fabulously wealthy by exerting **control** over who can use the **Windows operating system**. **Programmers** who develop **open-source code**, such as the **Linux software** used to run **computer servers**, tend not to be billionaires.

Economics operates at the **interface between these real and virtual sides of wealth**, which is mediated by **money**. The **money system** is a way to attach **virtual numbers** to **real goods and services**.

While the **prestige of economics** grew alongside this explosion

in material wealth, we should remember that the profession plays only a **supporting and explanatory role** – the **Industrial Revolution** was driven by **engineers**, not **economists**! And, as seen later, **economic growth** doesn't always translate into **broader measures of progress**.

ANCIENT ECONOMICS

The word "economics" is from the Greek oikos *(for "household") and* nomos *("law"), so means "household rule" or "home management".*

XENOPHON

One of the **first books** on the subject was by the **philosopher Xenophon** (431–c.360 BC), who was a contemporary of **Plato**. His tract ***Oikonomikos*** described "the business of the **good estate manager**". Writing in a time when Athens was growing rapidly in terms of both **size** and **complexity**, he argued that **complex tasks** are best approached through **division of labour** – an idea later championed by **Adam Smith**.

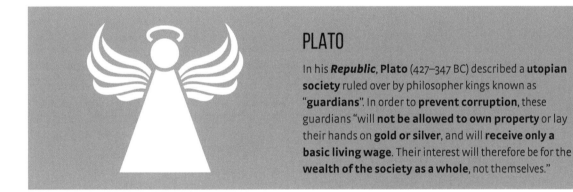

PLATO

In his ***Republic***, **Plato** (427–347 BC) described a **utopian society** ruled over by philosopher kings known as **"guardians"**. In order to **prevent corruption**, these guardians "will **not be allowed to own property** or lay their hands on **gold or silver**, and will **receive only a basic living wage**. Their interest will therefore be for the **wealth of the society as a whole**, not themselves."

ARISTOTLE

Plato's student **Aristotle** (384–322 BC) noticed that **merchants** often became **rich**, not through **producing anything of value themselves**, but simply through the **act of exchange**, or through **usury** (the **lending of money for interest**). In ***Politics***, he therefore distinguished between **two types of exchange**: the **"natural"** type that **aims to satisfy genuine needs**, and the **"unnatural"** that **aims only to make money**.

As we'll see, **ethical issues** such as **corruption** and **speculation** are still an important **challenge for economics**.

SCHOLASTIC ECONOMICS

In the Middle Ages, the school of economic thought known today as scholastic economics combined Aristotle's ideas with Christian theology, and focused on questions of ethics.

THE FIRST UNIVERSITIES

Aristotelean philosophy formed the core of the **curriculum** for the **first universities**, such as **Bologna** (founded in 1088), **Paris** (c.1150), and **Oxford** (1167).

ETHICAL QUESTIONS

Such questions are of course still very relevant. One study from 1986 asked the following question of a random sample of Canadians:

> **❝**A hardware store has been selling snow shovels for $15. The morning after a large snowstorm, the store raises the price to $20. Rate this action as: completely fair, acceptable, somewhat unfair, or very unfair.**❞**

AQUINAS

The Dominican friar Saint **Thomas Aquinas** (1225–74), who taught in **Paris** and **Cologne**, emphasized the **rationality of Greek philosophy**, writing that "**Reason** in man is rather like God in the world." He argued that **transactions** should be at a "**just price**" in the sense that neither the **buyer** nor the **seller** is **acting under duress**, or trying to **take advantage** of the other person.

Eighty-two per cent of the respondents chose "**somewhat unfair**" or "**very unfair**". **Consumers** don't like being **taken advantage of** any more today than they did in the Middle Ages.

FEUDALISM

Economics is always shaped by prevailing social structures and beliefs, and scholastic economics was in part a product of the feudal system in Europe, where what counted was not money, but land and power.

LORDS OF THE LAND

Sovereigns granted **land** to their **lords**, who in turn granted **plots** to their **vassals** in exchange for **work on the estate, military service**, and a **portion of the land's agricultural yield. Large areas** of land were reserved as **collectively managed commons** and were used for purposes such as **animal grazing** and **collecting firewood**. The **most powerful landlord** was the **Church**, which also dominated most of the thinking about **money** and **economics**.

ETHICS

The focus was not on **efficiency**, but on **ethics**. As **Thomas Aquinas** wrote, "**Charity** is the **mother of all virtues**, inasmuch as it informs all virtues." **Avarice** was treated as a **deadly sin**.

We no longer live in a **feudal system**, but many of the same concerns arise today. For example, the question of how to successfully **manage common areas**, e.g. the

Earth's atmosphere, has become especially **urgent** in recent times. And instead of **monopolistic landowners**, we have **monopolistic owners of intellectual property**, in what has been called **digital feudalism**.

Since the **Great Financial Crisis** of 2007/8, there have also been **increasing calls** for economics to **engage again with ethical issues**.

ISLAMIC ECONOMICS

As with the Christian Bible, sacred Islamic texts such as the Koran include statements that apply to the economy. Islamic law prohibits the trading of debt, the charging of interest, and gambling. Islam also requires every financial asset to be backed by a real asset.

IBN KHALDUN

The **founder of Islamic economics** is generally considered to be the scholar **Ibn Khaldun** (1332–1406). **Many of his ideas prefigure those of Adam Smith.**

For example, he showed how **division of labour** during a **harvest** creates **surplus value**: "Through **cooperation**, the **needs** of a **number of persons**, many times **greater than their own**, can be **satisfied**."

TAX POLICY

Khaldun is also credited with developing a version of a **labour theory of value** (discussed later), and the **theory of supply and demand**. His views on **tax policy** were even **paraphrased** by **Ronald Reagan**. As Khaldun wrote: "It should be known that at the **beginning of the dynasty, taxation yields a large revenue** from **small assessments**. At the **end of the dynasty**, taxation yields a **small revenue** from **large assessments**." Reagan added that "we're trying to get down to the **small assessments** and the **great revenues**".

Islamic finance gives a **different view** of our **modern financial system**, which involves the **trading of massive amounts of debt, charging of interest**, and **gambling on derivatives** that are **not backed by anything real**.

DOUBLE-ENTRY BOOKKEEPING

The growing role of money in the fifteenth century required a way to keep track of it. Having been used for over a century by merchants, the accounting method known as double-entry bookkeeping was codified by the mathematician and Franciscan friar Luca Pacioli, in his 1494 book Summa de arithmetica.

PROFITS

It also gave a **quick snapshot** of **profitability**. As Mr Micawber said in **Charles Dickens'** 1849 novel ***David Copperfield***: "Annual **income** £20, annual **expenditure** £19.19.6, result **happiness**. Annual **income** £20, annual **expenditure** £20.0.6, result **misery**."

ASSETS AND LIABILITIES

The technique is so named because **every transaction** is **entered in two different accounts**, once as a **debit** and once as a **credit**. For every **asset** on one side, there is a **liability** on the other.

The method helped **detect errors**, since the **sum of credits** over **all accounts** should be **balanced** by the **sum of debits**.

Of course, even with such **checks and balances**, **accountants** can still find ways to **cook the books**, or at least improve their flavour. One reason the UK travel firm **Thomas Cook** went bust in 2019 was because it was forced to **write off intangible assets** under the umbrella heading of "**goodwill**" to the tune of £1.1 billion.

MERCANTILISM

By the time of the Renaissance (fourteenth to seventeenth centuries), a doctrine known as mercantilism emerged, which was dedicated to building and maintaining the reach and power of nations – not so much by increasing economic activity, but by accumulating as much "treasure" as possible, in the form of precious metal.

USURY

Restrictions on usury were **gradually relaxed**. One result was the **rise of the bankers**, as epitomized by the phenomenally rich and powerful **Medici family** in Italy.

ZERO-SUM GAME

In this view, the **economy** was a **zero-sum game**. As **Thomas Mun** (1571–1641), who was a director of the **East India Company**, put it: **"One man's loss is another man's gain."** **Adam Smith** later wrote that the doctrine taught nations that **"their interest lies in beggaring all their neighbours"**.

Today, countries including the **US** and **China** are sometimes accused of pursuing **mercantilist, beggar-thy-neighbour trade policies**.

NEW WORLD

Technological advances in **shipping**, and **expeditions** by **explorers** such as **Columbus**, led to the establishment of **new trade routes** and an explosion in **world trade**. And the discovery of **apparently limitless supplies of gold and silver** in the **New World** meant that countries such as **Spain** suddenly found themselves flooded with **riches** (though **inflation** was a concern).

As **Columbus** wrote from Jamaica in 1503, **"Gold is a wonderful thing!** Whoever possesses it is master of everything he desires. With gold, one can even get souls into paradise."

THE INDUSTRIAL REVOLUTION

Prior to the mid-eighteenth century, human economic output had remained fairly stable. That changed with the Industrial Revolution, which saw the emergence of new manufacturing processes in Europe and the United States.

Industries affected include **textiles**, **chemicals**, **iron production**, **transportation**, and so on. The revolution touched **every aspect of people's lives**, but **especially the economy**.

MECHANIZATION

Hand production shifted to **steam-powered machines** and then to **mechanized factories**.

TIMELINE

- **1760** The textile industry in Great Britain begins to mechanize, leading to a vast increase in productivity
- **1781** James Watt patents an improved steam engine, which is soon used to power factories, steam boats, and trains
- **1793** The revolution crosses the Atlantic, as Samuel Slater opens the first textile mill in Rhode Island
- **1793** Eli Whitney invents the cotton gin, to mechanically separate cotton fibres from their seeds
- **1811** The Luddites attack factories in Great Britain to protest against the use of machinery

Mechanization led to **large increases in income and standards of living**, as well as an **increased rate of population growth**. There was also a **power shift** from those who **controlled land**, to those who **controlled capital**, in the forms of **machines** and **factories**.

NEW INSTITUTIONS

The Industrial Revolution also saw the development of **economic institutions** such as **trade unions**, which were **legalized in Great Britain** in 1824, and **corporate law**.

ADAM SMITH

Adam Smith championed a new approach to economics that emphasized free competition and economic growth. His ideas shaped the way we think about the capitalist economy.

 DATE 1723–90

 NATIONALITY SCOTTISH

 SCHOOL CLASSICAL ECONOMICS

 MAIN WORKS *THE THEORY OF MORAL SENTIMENTS; THE WEALTH OF NATIONS*

VALUE IS LABOUR

A basic question in economics is **what constitutes value**. For the **mercantilists**, value was **measured by a weight of precious metal**. But writing at the dawn of the Industrial Revolution, Smith realized that what counted was the **dynamics of exchange**. The value of **gold** or **silver** would **vary** with **factors** such as their **levels of production**, or **inflation**. While he agreed with the mercantilists that **price** was **measured in metal**, **value** was **determined by labour**.

REAL VERSUS NOMINAL

He therefore distinguished between **"nominal" prices**, and **"real" prices**, which **stripped out** such effects. As he wrote in his 1776 book ***The Wealth of Nations***, "The real price of every thing, what every thing really costs to the man who wants to acquire it, is the **toil and trouble of acquiring it**."

INFLUENCE ON THE US

The year 1776 was that of the **American revolution**. Smith's work exerted a **profound influence** on the **new government** there – and that influence **persists**.

The US economist **George Akerlof**, for example, describes the **"central ideology"** of the United States as conforming to "the **fundamental view of Adam Smith**", which even today "**drives huge amounts of policy**".

THE INVISIBLE HAND

Smith's most enduring idea – though the phrase appears just once in his The Wealth of Nations, *in a section on trade – was that of the "invisible hand" of the markets, which guides prices to their correct level. The term was later popularized by economist Paul Samuelson to explain Smith's vision of how markets work.*

NATURAL PRICE

According to this rule, the **price of an asset** is **automatically guided toward** its "**natural price**" (i.e. that which **corresponds to labour value**) by **market mechanisms**. If a particular good is **too expensive**, then **more suppliers will enter the market**, and **competition** will **drive the price down**. If the price is **too low**, then **suppliers will go broke** or **leave the market**, and the **price will go up**.

SELFISH GOOD

❝It is not from the benevolence of the butcher, the brewer, or the baker that we expect our dinner, but from their regard to their own interest. We address ourselves, not to their humanity but to their self-love, and never talk to them of our necessities but of their advantages.**❞**

Adam Smith,
The Wealth of Nations

Or, as **Samuelson** later paraphrased it in his 1948 *Economics*: "Every individual, in pursuing only his own **selfish good**, was led, as if by an **invisible hand**, to achieve the **best good for all**."

CLASSICAL ECONOMICS

Adam Smith is usually regarded as the founder of the school known as classical economics, which developed mostly in Britain.

CELEBRATED CLASSICAL ECONOMISTS

Some of the classical economists we will meet in later pages include:

- **Thomas Malthus** (1766–1834) – argued that **population growth** would be **limited by famine and disease**.

- **Jean-Baptiste Say** (1767–1832) – best known for **Say's law**, which states that "**Supply creates its own demand**" (though he never actually put it like that).

- **David Ricardo** (1772–1823) – formulated the **law of comparative advantage** in **international trade**.

- **John Stuart Mill** (1806–73) – leading proponent of **utilitarianism**.

MECHANISTIC LAWS

Like **Smith**, these thinkers saw **market economies** as being **driven by mechanistic laws** of **production** and **exchange**, and **self-regulated** by the **invisible hand**.

Wages rise and fall to account for **changes** in the **demand for labour**, while **interest rates adjust** to the **demand for capital**.

FREE TRADE

Unlike the mercantilists, the classical economists also favoured **free trade** between nations.

Their search for **mechanistic rules** was inspired in part by the successes of **Newtonian physics**. The **invisible hand** was the **economics equivalent** of a **law of gravity**, which **drove prices** to their **natural level**.

At the same time, the classical economists saw an **important role** for the **state**, for example in preventing the formation of **monopolies** and maintaining the conditions for **free competition**.

KARL MARX

The German philosopher and economist Karl Marx believed that social injustices – of the sort that were very much on display in Victorian factories and slums – were an inherent feature of capitalism that would eventually lead to its demise.

 DATE 1818–83

 NATIONALITY GERMAN

 SCHOOL MARXIST ECONOMICS

 MAIN WORKS *THE COMMUNIST MANIFESTO,* WRITTEN IN 1848 WITH FRIEDRICH ENGELS, AND *DAS KAPITAL* (FIRST VOLUME PUBLISHED IN 1867)

WORKERS VERSUS OWNERS

In Marx's view, **society** was **divided into two opposing classes**: the **capitalists**, who **own the means of production**, and the **labourers**, who have **no wealth** apart from that **produced by their labour**. The **wealthy capitalists** have a more **powerful** position than labourers so can **dictate wages and working conditions**.

SURPLUS VALUE

Marx was strongly influenced by the classical economists. In fact he introduced the term "classical economist" in order to distinguish them from their "vulgar" successors. Like **Adam Smith**, Marx saw labour as the **ultimate source of value**; however, in **capitalism** there was a **gap** between the **value produced by labourers** and the **wages** they received. This "**surplus value**" was **unjustly captured** by the capitalist as **profit**.

REVOLUTION

Marx argued that, over time, capital would become **increasingly concentrated**, leading to the **exploitation** and **alienation** of workers. This process would ultimately lead to **revolution**. As he put it in *Das Kapital*: "The knell of capitalist **private property** sounds. The **expropriators are expropriated**."

THE MARGINAL REVOLUTION

At the same time that Marx was outlining the collapse of capitalism, a generation of younger economists was launching a rather different "marginal revolution", which would form the basis for today's mainstream theory.

MARGINAL UTILITY

The **marginal revolution** dates back to the early 1870s, when **William Stanley Jevons** in **England**, **Leon Walras** in **France**, and **Carl Menger** in **Austria** independently arrived at the conclusion that **value** should be **measured not by labour**, as the **classical economists** had asserted, but instead by **utility** – or, to be more exact, by **marginal utility**.

HEDONISTIC CALCULUS

The concept of utility dates to the philosopher **Jeremy Bentham** (1748–1832), who defined it as the **quality that increases a person's happiness**. It could be **calculated** according to the **pseudo-Newtonian "hedonistic calculus"**:

""Sum up all the values of all the pleasures on the one side, and those of all the pains on the other. The balance, if it be on the side of pleasure, will give the good tendency of the act upon the whole, with respect to the interests of that individual person; if on the side of pain, the bad tendency of it upon the whole.**"**

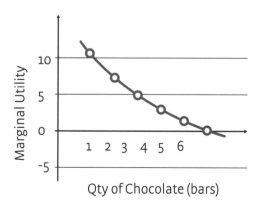

Marginal utility takes into account one's **current state**, so for example the utility of a tenth glass of water is probably less than the utility of the first (an example of **diminishing marginal utility**).

NEOCLASSICAL ECONOMICS

Utility theory suggested that the economy could be modelled mathematically using "a mechanics of utility and self-interest" similar to Newtonian mechanics. This physics-inspired approach became known as neoclassical economics.

A REAL SCIENCE

This **switch from labour to utility** was motivated in part by the **growing influence** of **finance** and **international trade** on **price**, which was not consistent with the **classical labour theory of value**. However, it was also driven by the desire to put the subject onto a **firmly scientific footing**.

As **Jevons** wrote, "if Economics is to be a **real science** at all, it must not deal merely with **analogies**; it must reason by **real equations**, like all the **other sciences** which have reached at all a **systematic character**".

MEASURING UTILITY

Utility was viewed as the **social equivalent of energy**, measured in units of "**utils**". Of course, it is **no easier to measure utility than it is to measure labour**, but **Jevons** argued that it can be **measured indirectly through price**.

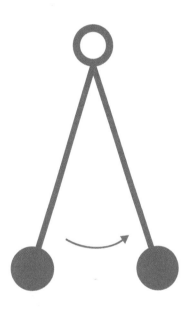

> **❝** We can no more know nor measure gravity in its own nature than we can measure a feeling; but, just as we measure gravity by its effects in the motion of a pendulum, so we may estimate the equality or inequality of feelings by the decisions of the human mind. The will is our pendulum, and its oscillations are minutely registered in the price lists of the markets. **❞**

WIlliam Stanley Jevons

ALFRED MARSHALL

Perhaps the most influential neoclassical economist was Alfred Marshall, whose 1890 Principles of Economics *was still being used as a textbook in economics classes as late as the 1950s.*

 DATE 1842–1924

 NATIONALITY ENGLISH

 SCHOOL NEOCLASSICAL ECONOMICS

 MAIN WORKS *PRINCIPLES OF ECONOMICS* (1890)

SUPPLY AND DEMAND

Marshall's textbook **combined a number of key ideas into a coherent whole**, including **marginal utility, supply and demand, elasticity, economic surplus**, and so on. Many of these ideas could be illustrated using a **diagram** that (as discussed in more detail later) shows how **supply and demand vary with price**. The **demand curve** slopes **down**, since, as Marshall argued, **consumer demand** normally **decreases with price**, while the **supply curve** slopes **up**. Marshall likened the two lines to the **two blades of a pair of scissors**, which combine to give **price**.

PARTIAL EQUILIBRIUM

The **point at which the two curves intersect** represented the **equilibrium price**, at which **supply perfectly matched demand** and the **market clears**. This was called a **partial equilibrium analysis** because it considered **only one market** for a particular good. The problem of how many **interlinked markets** come to an **equilibrium** was later tackled by **Léon Walras**.

Marshall also **popularized** the use of the word "**economics**" as a replacement for "**political economy**" to describe the field.

MATHEMATICAL BIOLOGY

In the preface to his textbook Marshall wrote that "**the Mecca of the economist lies in economic biology**", however "**biological conceptions are more complex than those of mechanics**; a volume on Foundations must therefore give a relatively large place to **mechanical analogies**, and frequent use is made of the term **equilibrium**."

CARL MENGER

A separate strand of marginal utility theory was developed by the Austrian economist Carl Menger.

 DATE 1840–1921

 NATIONALITY AUSTRIAN

 SCHOOL AUSTRIAN ECONOMICS

 MAIN WORKS *PRINCIPLES OF ECONOMICS* (1871)

SUBJECTIVE VALUE

Unlike **Bentham**, **Menger** did not believe that **utility** was something that could be **measured objectively** in terms of "**utils**". His **subjective theory of value** instead held that utility is **subjective** and **depends on the person**, so **only individuals can decide what is best for them**.

Economics therefore needed to focus not on **groups** or **aggregates**, but on **individuals**, who are the **only ones** who can **act** and make **decisions**.

ENABLING TRADE

The fact that an **amount of money** is **exchanged** for a **quantity of goods** does not mean the two are **somehow equivalent**. Instead the whole **point of trade** is to allow people to **exchange goods** that they have for things they **need or value more**, so **both sides gain**. **Middlemen** provide an **important service** by **bringing buyers and sellers together**.

INSTITUTIONS

Menger argued that **social institutions**, including the **use of money** and **language**, arise **organically** as a **solution to human needs**, so do not need to be **consciously designed** or **planned**.

Menger was a founder of the **Austrian School of economics**, which, as we'll see later, has remained **influential**.

MARGINAL PRODUCTIVITY

In the United States, the economist John Bates Clark (1847–1938) applied the marginal utility theory to the problem of earnings and productivity.

NATURAL LAW

The result of Clark's analysis was that people **earn what they make**. Or as he put it in his 1899 work ***The Distribution of Wealth***, "The **distribution of income** to society is controlled by a **natural law** ... this law, if it worked **without friction**, would give to **every agent of production** the **amount of wealth which that agent creates**."

THE LONG TERM

Of course, this **equilibrium** was only attained over the **long term**, and there would be **short-term fluctuations** where workers would be **paid too much** or **too little**. He explained the idea using the **metaphor of waves on an ocean**: "The surface, considering its size, shows only **trifling irregularities**." However, "If we take a bird's-eye view ... we may treat waves and currents as **minor aberrations** due to '**disturbing causes**.'"

FAIR WAGE?

Clark's finding was convenient for **supporters of capitalism**, especially since the **United States** at the time was being rocked by **social ferment** that was inspired in part by **Marx**'s rather different theories.

Economists later modified Clark's theory to account for factors such as **human capital** (for example, **education**), but, as we'll see, the question of **what constitutes a fair wage** is still very much in dispute.

INFLATION

Inflation occurs when prices in general go up, so that money loses its purchasing power. While inflation is a complex phenomenon, a basic cause is that there is too much money chasing too few goods.

QUANTITY THEORY

This **quantity theory of money**, as it became known, was later developed by the American economist **Irving Fisher** (1867–1947) in his **equation of exchange**. This states that $MV = PT$, where M is the **amount of money in circulation**, V is the **average rate** (or **velocity**) at which the **money changes hands**, P is the **average transaction price**, and T is the **total volume of transactions**.

The left side of the equation simply counts the **total flow of money** – if a pound coin changes hands three times in a year, it represents a total of £3 in **transactions**. The right-hand side, meanwhile, counts the **amount of money spent on buying things**.

 $$M V = P T$$

CONTROLLING INFLATION

Fisher argued that V and T are **fixed**, so the **average price** P has to be **proportional** to the **amount of money** M.

So to **control inflation**, you just need to **control the money supply**, as **Copernicus** said. (As will become clear later, it **isn't quite that simple**.)

As the Polish astronomer **Copernicus** (1473–1543) put it, while advising the King of Poland: "It is my conclusion that **money usually depreciates when it becomes too abundant**."

His observation was backed up by the so-called "**Price Revolution**" which saw prices in Western Europe gain due to the **influx of gold** from **the New World**.

DEFLATION

Deflation is the opposite of inflation: instead of prices rising, they fall.

GOLD STANDARD

During the **gold standard era**, deflation was a **regular event**, as **the supply of new gold** would sometimes **fall behind the rate of economic growth**.

UK inflation averaged only 0.4 per cent a year over the **six centuries** between 1300 and 1900. **Two centuries** – the fifteenth and nineteenth – experienced **average annual deflation** of 0.1 per cent and 0.4 per cent respectively.

In the **US**, the **last three decades of the nineteenth century** saw **average annual deflation** of -1.5 per cent, as the economy adjusted to **advances** in **technology** and **transportation**, and the country switched from a **bimetallic silver/gold standard** to **gold alone**, resulting in a **shortage of coin**.

GREAT DEPRESSION

A **little deflation** might seem like a **good thing**, especially if it occurs during a time of **economic growth**. However, during the **Great Depression** years of 1929 to 1933, **prices** in the US fell by 24 per cent at the same time that **GDP** fell in **real terms** by 30 per cent. In cases such as this, deflation creates a **positive feedback loop**, where people **withhold from making purchases** because they think **prices will drop in the future**, which in turn **slows economic activity** and **exacerbates deflation**.

Deflation is particularly dangerous at times of **high debt**, because while the **price** of something like a house **may erode**, the **debt** on the house **doesn't**.

THE MONEY ILLUSION

The "money illusion" is our tendency to think in terms of nominal values rather than real, inflation-adjusted values.

FISHER EQUATION

The so-called **Fisher equation** states that if the **nominal** or **observed interest rate** is n, and the **rate of inflation** is i, then the **real interest rate** is $r = n - i$. Real interest rates may therefore be **lower than they appear**, if you don't **strip out** inflation.

The money illusion also makes it **hard to connect past costs with present costs** – for example, to understand whether **selling your house** for **double what you paid** was a **great deal** – or for **businesses** to **raise prices** without **losing customers**.

NO INFLATION HERE

Fisher was very famous in his day, writing and lecturing on a variety of subjects, including the **stock market**. However, his **reputation** – and his **personal wealth** – took something of a hit in the **Great Crash** of 1929. Just days before it started, he had asserted that "**security values in most instances were not inflated**" and months later he continued to assure **investors** that it was all just a **blip**.

The **Dow Jones index** eventually **lost 89 per cent of its value**. It turned out that **most of the money that investors thought they had made** was actually an **illusion**.

RATIONAL ECONOMIC MAN

Microeconomics focuses on individual transactions. At its core is the concept of rational economic man – or Homo economicus, *as he is also known – who has long enjoyed a leading role in economic theory.*

SELF-INTEREST

Neoclassical economists assumed in their **models** that people act with **machine-like rationality** in order to **maximize their own utility**. As the English economist **Francis Edgeworth** put it in his *Mathematical Psychics* (1881), "The **first principle** of economics is that every agent is actuated only by **self-interest**."

THE UNIVERSAL BOGEY

Obviously *Homo economicus* was something of a **caricature**, and no sooner was he born than economists began to **distance themselves** from him. As the English economist **Lionel Robbins** put it in 1932, "if it were generally realized that Economic Man is only an expository device ... it is improbable that he would be such a **universal bogey**".

CLAIRVOYANT

However, **rational economic man** continued to play a key role in **economic theorizing**. He reached perhaps his **most extreme form**, with god-like abilities to look into the future, in the 1950s proof of the **First Welfare theorem** – or the "**invisible hand theorem**" as it is also known – which claimed that **free markets**, if **left to their own devices**, would reach a kind of **stable and optimal equilibrium**.

Today, the concept of rational economic man still plays an important role in **economic models**, but is **increasingly questioned** by **behavioural economists**, and **feminist economists who see it as gendered**.

THE CORPORATION

Rational economic man is obviously not a realistic model of human behaviour. However, there is one entity that seems designed to approximate his behaviour: the corporation.

LIMITED LIABILITY

Corporations have **limited liability**, which means that an **investor** in the corporation **does not share responsibility for its debts or other obligations**. When corporations were first established in the early 1800s, this was a **special status** used as a carrot to get people to invest in **risky ventures** such as **insurance** or **canal building**, but it **soon became commonplace**.

CORPORATE PERSONHOOD

In 1886, the **US Supreme Court** also ruled that a corporation has a **legal status** of "**corporate personhood**", which gives them some of the **rights of people**, including **freedom of speech**.

SHAREHOLDER PRIMACY

In the 1919 case of **Dodge *v* Ford Motor Company**, the **Michigan Supreme Court** ruled that **Henry Ford** had to operate the **Ford Motor Company** in the **interests of its shareholders**, rather than those of its **customers or employees**. This case led to the idea of "**shareholder primacy**".

As **Milton Friedman** put it in 1962: "Few trends could so thoroughly **undermine the very foundations** of our **free society** as the acceptance by **corporate officials** of a **social responsibility** other than to **make as much money for their stockholders as possible**."

PREFERENCES

No one, including rational economic man, can optimize their own utility unless they know what they want. Economists therefore assumed that people have a fixed set of preferences.

CARDINAL UTILITY

Preferences can be **modelled** in a number of different ways. One approach, known as **cardinal** (as in **fundamental**) **utility theory**, assumes that utility is something that can be expressed as a **magnitude**, such as a number of "**utils**". This was the approach of **Jeremy Bentham** and the early **neoclassical economists**. It is now considered largely **out of date**, but still has a role in areas such as **decision-making under risk**.

ORDINAL UTILITY

As neoclassical economics developed, economists including **Vilfredo Pareto** and later **Paul Samuelson** realized that their theories only needed people to be able to **rank their preferences in order**, which is the **ordinal approach to utility** (from the Latin *ordo* for "order").

REVEALED PREFERENCE

Economists also speak about **revealed preference**. The idea here is that **what counts is not what people say, but what they do**. We can therefore **infer utility** by watching **how much people will pay** for something.

In **standard economic models**, **preferences** are assumed to be **constant**. However, in reality they **change** with **time** and with **context**. If they didn't then **marketers** would be **out of a job**.

DIMINISHING MARGINAL UTILITY

The so-called "law of diminishing marginal utility" states that the utility a consumer receives per unit of a commodity decreases with the number of units obtained.

EVERYTHING HAS ITS LIMIT

As an extreme case, if your TV is broken, then **buying a replacement** is **useful**; buying **two** is **over the top**. The **first glass of wine** is **enjoyable**, the **fifth** may lead to a **hangover**. More generally, there will be a **limit on how much of an item is useful**, and as we approach that limit the **marginal utility will decrease**.

DIMINISHING RETURNS

The same idea applies to **production**. If a **factory** asks its **workers** to **work twice as long**, their **productivity is likely to suffer**. If instead it **doubles its workforce**, it probably **won't produce twice as much**, because the factory will become **overcrowded**. This principle is called the "**law of diminishing returns**".

ECONOMIES OF SCALE

As seen below, these "**laws**" were **important assumptions** for **classical economists** to make, in order to make sense of the **dynamics of supply and demand**. However, as they knew, there are **many exceptions**. For example, **economies of scale** mean that **price per unit of production** often **declines the more that is produced**. And in the **digital economy**, it takes **as much work to produce a single copy of a software program** as it does to produce an **unlimited number**.

DEMAND

Demand refers to people's desire to purchase a good, which is measured in terms of the quantity required.

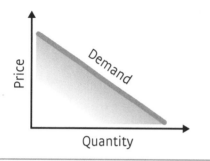

DEMAND CURVE

Because it **varies with price**, **demand** is usually expressed as a **theoretical curve**, showing **how much of the good** is **demanded** at **each price**. Demand curves can be for an **individual person**, or represent a sum over a **large number of people**, in which case it is called an **aggregate demand curve**.

DOWNWARD SLOPE

The graph usually **slopes down**, because when **prices fall** the **demand generally increases**. For an **individual**, **diminishing marginal utility** also means that **demand decreases with quantity**. **Exceptions** include things like **luxury items**, where people may demand a good exactly **because it is expensive**.

DEMAND SHIFTS

One way to **change demand** for a good is to **change the price** – for example, reduce it in a sale. However, demand can also shift due to some **change in the market**, such as a **recession**.

DEMAND ELASTICITY

The **slope of the curve** is related to the **elasticity of demand**. **Inelastic goods** include **necessities** such as **food staples** or **medication**, or goods where there is **no easy substitute**. So-called **discretionary items**, such as a **movie ticket**, might be more **price-sensitive** and therefore **elastic**.

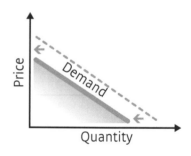

DEMAND-SIDE ECONOMICS

Since consumer demand **supports much of the economy**, **government policy-makers** put a lot of effort into trying to **manipulate demand**, either through **fiscal policy** (i.e. **government spending**) or **monetary policy** (**tuning interest rates**).

SUPPLY

Supply refers to the quantity of goods that producers bring to market.

SUPPLY CURVE

Like the **demand curve**, the **supply curve** is another **tool from classical economics** that is **still used** by economists today (though as we'll see, **both curves suffer from a measurement problem**). Again, the curve can apply to an **individual firm**, or to an **industry as a whole**.

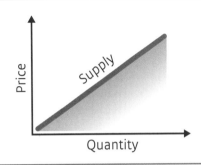

UPWARDS SLOPE

Supply curves are usually shown **sloping up**, meaning that **supply increases with price** and **vice versa**. For an **individual firm**, the **"law" of diminishing returns** suggests that if the firm **scales up its operation** to take on extra work, it becomes **less efficient**, so **prices have to go up**. At the **aggregate level**, **higher prices** would on the other hand **draw more producers into the market**, **increasing supply**.

SUPPLY ELASTICITY

The **elasticity of supply** is again related to the **slope of the curve**. The case of a **digital good** produced at **no extra cost** would have **infinite elasticity**.

SUPPLY SHIFT

Like demand, supply depends on **factors other than price**, such as the **costs of production**, and the **general state of the economy**. For example, **technological innovation** might boost the **rate of production** and **shift the entire supply curve** to the right.

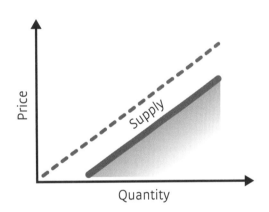

SUPPLY-SIDE ECONOMICS

Just as **policy-makers** sometimes try to **stimulate demand**, a **supply-side approach** would try to **increase supply** by **cutting the tax and regulatory burdens** on **companies** and **consumers**.

ELASTICITIES

A key notion from classical economics that is still used in economic theory is that of elasticity, which refers to sensitivity to changes in economic variables.

PRICE

As seen already, **price elasticity** measures how much the **quantity of a good** that is **supplied** or **demanded** varies with **changes in price**. Suppose we change the price by a **set amount**, say 10 per cent. If in this case the **change in quantity** is **greater** than 10 per cent, the good is termed **price elastic**; if the change is **less** than 10 per cent, the good would be **price inelastic**.

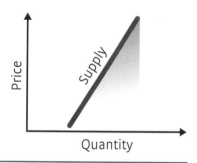

INCOME

Another kind of elasticity is **income elasticity**. This measures how **demand increases when income goes up**. **Luxury goods** are **income elastic**, because demand is strongly **dependent on income**.

CROSS-ELASTICITY

Finally, **cross-elasticity of demand** measures how the **quantity demanded for one good** is affected by a **change in price for another good**. For example, if the **demand for fuel-efficient cars increases** with the **cost of fuel**, the cross-elasticity will be **positive**. In this case the goods are called **substitutes** (you can **spend more money** on **fuel**, or on the **fuel-efficient car**). If the cross-elasticity is **negative**, then the goods are called **complementary**.

SUBSTITUTION

Elasticity of substitution measures how easily one **production cost** can be **exchanged** for another – for example, **firing workers** and **replacing them with robots**.

WARNING

The **concept of elasticity** assumes that the **relationship between economic variables** is **approximately linear**, which as discussed later is **not always the case**.

THE LAW OF SUPPLY AND DEMAND

Putting the supply and demand curves together gives the "law of supply and demand".

GRAPHICAL REPRESENTATION

While the idea of **supply and demand curves** was first developed by the French mathematician and economist **Antoine Augustin Cournot** (1801–77), the figure used today is based on one published in 1870 by the engineering professor **Fleeming Jenkin** (1833–85).

This graph, with its **downward-sloping demand** and **upward-sloping supply**, was **popularized** by the neoclassical economist **Alfred Marshall** (it is sometimes called the **Marshallian cross**) and still features in **introductory textbooks**. It also plays a **key role** in the **mathematical models of the economy** used to make **policy decisions**.

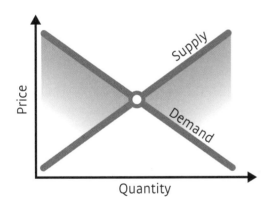

OPTIMAL BALANCE

The **"law of supply and demand"** states that **supply and demand intersect** at a **unique point of equilibrium** where the **market clears**, and **net utility is maximized**. **Producing more** than this amount will **destroy value** because the **price will be lower** than the **cost of production**.

The figure can therefore be viewed as a **graphical version** of **Adam Smith's invisible hand**, where the **actions of consumers and producers drive prices to a stable point** that reflects **intrinsic value**.

IDENTIFIABILITY

One problem is that **supply and demand curves cannot be separately measured**, because all we have is **transactions**, which **depend on both supply and demand at the same time** (in **mathematics**, this is called the **identifiability problem**). The graph must therefore be viewed as a **theoretical construct**.

EQUILIBRIUM

A key assumption in both classical and neoclassical economics is that market forces drive prices to a stable equilibrium.

CETERIS PARIBUS

This **equilibrium** is **assumed to hold** *ceteris paribus* or "**other things being equal**". (This phrase is often used in economics to indicate that some **relationship between two variables holds true so long as nothing else changes**.) However, the **equilibrium will adjust** if **something external** happens to **shift the demand or supply curves**.

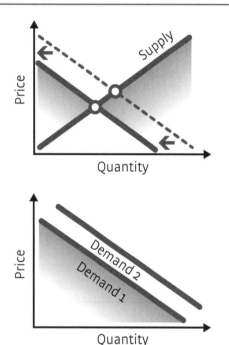

DEMAND SHIFT

Suppose that **government spending** succeeds in **shifting the demand curve to the right**, but the **supply curve stays in the same place**. Then the **equilibrium point** shifts to one of **higher demand**, and also **higher price**.

SUPPLY SHIFT

If instead there is a **decrease in supply**, because producers are **cutting back**, then the **supply curve shifts to the left**, but this time the **demand curve stays in the same place**. The **equilibrium point** therefore shifts to one of **lower demand**, but the **price is again higher**.

A **change in prices** can therefore be due to **very different economic forces** being at play.

COMPLEXITY

While the **supply and demand diagram** implies the existence of a **stable equilibrium price**, the fact that **supply and demand affect each other** can lead to extremely **complex behaviour**. **Complexity scientists** argue that some systems, such as the **stock market**, are best seen as being in a state that is **far from equilibrium**.

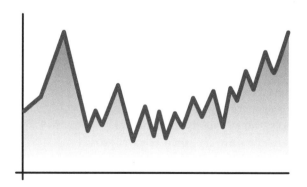

PRICE CONTROLS

Price controls are sometimes used by governments to keep prices at what they see as a reasonable level.

MINIMUM WAGE

Most **industrialized countries** set a **minimum wage**, which acts as a **lower bound** on what **firms can pay their workers**. The intention is to avoid **exploitation of workers**.

RENT CONTROL

Another example is **rent controls**. Governments sometimes **cap rents**, or cap the **rate at which prices are allowed to increase each year** during a tenancy.

MARKET DISTORTIONS?

Economists have traditionally tended to see such **well-intentioned interventions** as **distortions to the optimal equilibrium**.

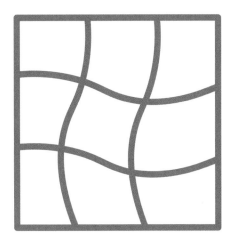

ECONOMIC STIMULUS

However, **analysis is complicated**, because **raising wages** or **limiting rents** can also be seen as a kind of **economic stimulus**, which **puts money into the pockets of lower-paid people**, who are especially likely to **spend it rather than save**. Some **empirical studies**, for example, suggest that a **realistic minimum wage** can even have a **net positive effect on employment**.

According to the **law of supply and demand**, **artificially boosting** the **price of labour** will lead to a **decline in the demand for labour**. And **rent controls** may mean that **landlords prefer to sell their properties**, thus **decreasing the rental supply**.

INDIFFERENCE CURVE

An indifference curve is a plot showing quantities of two goods,
where each point on the curve has the same utility.

IT'S ALL THE SAME

A consumer will therefore be **indifferent** to **any combination of goods** represented by the curve. These plots were first developed by **neoclassical economists**, including **Vilfredo Pareto**.

PERFECT SUBSTITUTION

Suppose that an **ounce of gold** costs **fifty times more** than an **ounce of silver**. If we say that the **utility** of the latter is 1, then the **utility of an ounce of gold** is 50. A **total utility** of 10 could then be achieved by holding:

Gold	Silver
0	10
0.05	7.5
0.1	5
0.15	2.5
0.2	0

which when plotted is a straight line.

MIXED BAG

For this example, the goods were assumed to be **perfect substitutes** for one another. More often, people will want to have a **mix of both goods**. In this case the graph will be **convex to the origin**, reflecting the **greater utility of a combination**.

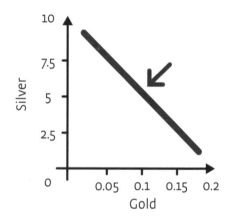

The **slope of the curve** represents the **willingness of the consumer** to make a **trade-off between the goods**.

As with **supply and demand curves, indifference curves** can be constructed for **individuals**, or **aggregated over a group**.

CRITICISM

The use of **indifference curves** allowed economists to base their models on **ranked preferences rather than measurements of utility**. However, the problem remains that, as with supply and demand curves, **indifference curves are theoretical constructs**. As **Joseph Schumpeter** observed in 1954: "From a practical standpoint we are not much better off when drawing **purely imaginary indifference curves** than we are when speaking of **purely imaginary utility functions**."

CONSUMER BUDGET

The consumer budget is the total amount a consumer has to spend.

THE BUDGET LINE

If we plot a number of **convex** indifference curves for **different total levels of utility**, we get a **set of nested curves which don't intersect**. Suppose that the **consumer** has a **set total budget** for the two items. It can be **added to the plot** as a **straight line sloping downwards. Any point on this line has the same cost**.

The **indifference curve** that is **tangent to this budget line** then **intersects** it at the point representing the **optimal balance of the two goods** for this consumer, since **any other point** on the budget line will have **less total utility**.

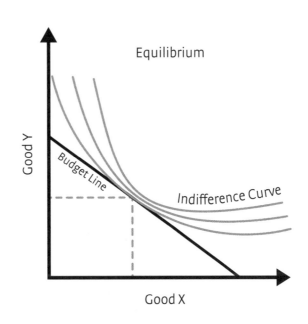

Equilibrium

Good Y

Budget Line

Indifference Curve

Good X

OPTIMAL EQUILIBRIUM

This point, known as the **optimal equilibrium point**, also **corresponds to the point** at which the **marginal utility of each good** (i.e. the **utility** of the last dollar spent on it) is **equal**.

DEMAND

The **demand** for a good at a **particular price** corresponds to the **optimal equilibrium point** found by **comparing that good with a composite of all other goods** (so the **choice** is **spending** the money **on that good** or on **other stuff**). In theory at least, this process could be used to construct a **demand curve**.

ECONOMIC SURPLUS

The consumer surplus is the difference between the price a consumer would pay, and the one they actually pay.

CONSUMER SURPLUS

Suppose that you buy ten items of some good. The fact that the **demand curve normally slopes down** means that you **would have bought** the first item at a **higher price**. Since the price you **actually pay** is the **lower price**, this means that in principle you are **getting a deal** on the first item, and also the second, and so on.

PRODUCER SURPLUS

Similarly, the fact that the **supply curve normally slopes up** means that in principle producers **would have sold** the first item at a **lower cost**. They therefore make a **producer surplus** when they sell you ten items. This surplus feeds into the **company profit**.

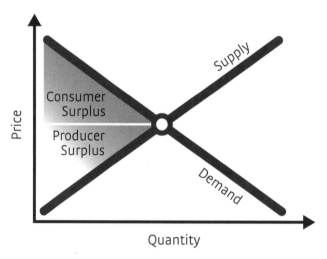

The **economic surplus** – also known as **total welfare** or **Marshallian surplus** (after **Alfred Marshall**) – is just the **sum of the consumer and producer surpluses**, for the **economy as a whole**. It gives an idea of the **total gains** that emerge from **production** and **trade**.

Classical economists saw this surplus as being used by people in a manner that depended on **class**: **labourers** used it for **subsistence**, **capitalists** to **invest**, and **landlords** to **support their lifestyle**.

If there **weren't any economic surplus**, then presumably **trade** would **grind to a halt**. The aim of **marketers** is to **turn consumer surplus into producer surplus**, by **coaxing consumers into paying the maximum**.

DEADWEIGHT LOSSES

Government actions such as price controls or taxes shift the supply and demand diagram and can create a deadweight loss that reduces the total economic surplus.

TAX

For example, a **carbon tax** on **gasoline** will **increase costs** and therefore **shift the supply curve vertically**. The **total surplus** now consists of the **producer surplus**, the **consumer surplus**, and the **tax revenue**. However, as seen in the figure, the total surplus is **lower than it would have been without the tax**. The **missing portion** is referred to as the **deadweight loss**, and occurs because the **total amount of trade** has been **lowered by the tax**. It is called **deadweight** because it **doesn't represent a gain for any party in the transaction** (except in this case the planet).

What seems like a **deadweight loss** from the point of view of **economic efficiency** can sometimes make the system more **robust**.

The estimated deadweight loss depends on the (theoretical) **shapes** of the **demand and supply curves**, so is affected by things like **elasticity**.

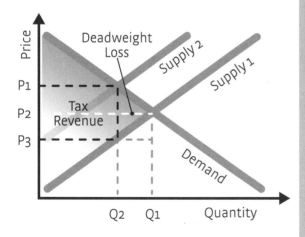

CAUSES

Deadweight losses can be **caused by other factors** such as **monopolies**, **price controls**, **tariffs**, **quotas**, **subsidies**, and so on. A different kind of deadweight loss occurs when **prices are artificially low** because they **don't cover** the **actual costs of production**. For example, if a factory doesn't **dispose of its waste** properly, then it is effectively **undercutting the price**.

According to one 1993 paper, the **Christmas season** is an **archetypal example of a deadweight loss**, because of all the **wasteful spending on gifts**. No wonder it is called the **dismal science**.

OPPORTUNITY COST

Opportunity cost is the loss of potential gain that occurs when we make a choice. For example, you have chosen to read this book, when you could be usefully employed making money (unless of course you are reading it while at work!).

PARABLE OF THE BROKEN WINDOW

Although he didn't use the term "opportunity cost", the concept was developed by the French economist **Frédéric Bastiat** (1801–50), who illustrated it with his **parable of the broken window**.

The parable concerns a shopkeeper whose window is broken by a small boy. Thirty people tell him that, while it's a shame he **will have to spend six francs repairing it**, at least it is **good news for the glazier**.

As Bastiat points out though: "It is not seen that, as our shopkeeper has **spent six francs upon one thing**, he **cannot spend them upon another**. It is not seen that if he had not had a **window to replace**, he would, perhaps, have replaced his **old shoes**, or added another **book** to his library. In short, **he would have employed his six francs in some way**, which this accident has **prevented**."

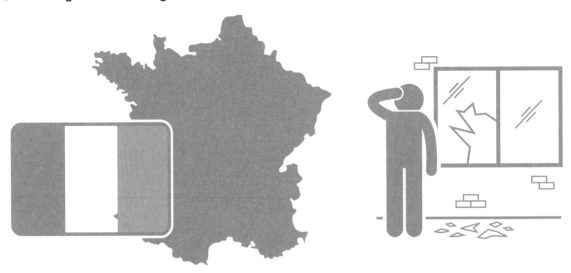

NATURAL DISASTERS

A **similar phenomenon** occurs when **natural disasters** appear to **boost the economy** by **stimulating reconstruction**.

PERFECT COMPETITION

Implicit in the idea that market pressures drive price to an optimum equilibrium is the assumption of perfect competition.

CONDITIONS

Conditions include:

- **Products** are **homogeneous**, so one **supplier's** are **indistinguishable** from **those of another**.
- There are many **producers** and **consumers**, and none are **large** or **powerful** enough to **control the price** – they are **price takers**, rather than **price setters**.
- No **artificial barriers to entry** for **new firms**, or **distortions** due to **government interference**.

- Everyone has **access** to **perfect information** about the **state of the market**.
- **Buyers act rationally** to **optimize their utility**, and **sellers** to **maximize their profits**.
- **Transaction costs** are **zero**.
- People are **free to move** where they want, **at no cost**.

NORMAL PROFIT

The result of these **competitive pressures** is that firms only earn a so-called "**normal profit**", which is just the **cost of doing business in a sustainable way**. The **market** is "**allocatively efficient**" in the sense that **marginal revenue** (i.e. the **revenue** from an **additional unit of output**) is **equal to the market price**, so **production perfectly represents consumer preferences**.

Of course **no such perfect market actually exists**. Perhaps the **closest thing** is the market for a **commodity such as wheat**, where there are many **individual farmers** supplying a **fairly uniform product** to a **large market**; or the market for **foreign currencies**. (Ironically, **both of these markets** tend to be rather **unstable**.) In economics it is therefore usually interpreted as a kind of **aspirational standard**, against which **real markets are compared**.

EFFICIENCY

In physics or engineering, the efficiency of a process equals the ratio of the useful work performed to the total amount of energy consumed – but in economics, the term is used in a number of different ways, usually to describe a property of perfectly competitive markets.

ALLOCATIVE EFFICIENCY

This means that the **price** (which should measure the **benefits to consumers** of **what they are buying**) is **equal to the costs of producing the marginal units**.

PRODUCTIVE EFFICIENCY

This means that **goods are produced with no waste**. In the **long run**, goods in a **perfectly competitive market** are **produced** and **sold** at the **lowest possible cost**. If firms **charge more**, then **competitors enter** and **take their business**; if they **don't charge enough**, they **go bust**.

PARETO EFFICIENCY

This was named after the neoclassical economist **Vilfredo Pareto**, and refers to a **situation where nothing can be changed without making at least one person worse off**. This is a rather technical statement, since in real life **most changes involve winners or losers**, but it plays a **major role** in **economic theorizing**.

EFFICIENT MARKETS

Finally, there is the **efficient market hypothesis**, which states that **assets are correctly priced**, at least in the sense that **no one can come up with a more accurate valuation than that of the markets**.

MARKET FAILURE

Market failure is an umbrella term for reasons that markets might not allocate resources efficiently.

CAUSES OF MARKET FAILURE

Causes of market failure include:

- **Abuse of market power**, as in a **monopoly**.
- **Costs** such as **pollution**, called **externalities**, that are **not borne by the market**.
- **Supplying public goods** that are for the **benefit of all** (this is why lighthouses are usually run by the state).
- **Imperfect information**, which **affects people's ability to make optimal decisions**.

GOVERNMENT FAILURE

Governments can try to **correct these failures** through **regulations**, **taxes**, **subsidies**, or **other policy measures**. On the other hand, they can **cause their own kind of market failure**, sometimes known as **government failure**.

An example is when the government tries to **manipulate the economy** by **setting inappropriate price controls**, or **"crowds out" private investment** by **allocating its own resources** in an **inefficient way**. Governments are also affected by **cronyism**, **corruption**, and the **desire to manipulate the economy** for **short-term electoral gains**.

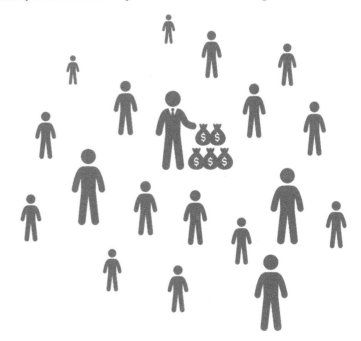

The term **"market failure"** is a little **loaded** because it implies that in a **natural state** markets would be **perfectly competitive**, which isn't the case if – as some economists argue – markets actually **tend rather naturally toward inequality**, with **market power** and **access to information** becoming increasingly **concentrated**.

MONOPOLY

At the other end of the competition spectrum from perfect competition we have the monopoly, where there is only a single supplier, with complete control over what it charges.

MARKET CONTROL

If a company has a monopoly it will usually **opt to raise the price** while **restricting the supply**. This allows it to **make more money** while doing **less work**.

Sometimes a monopoly is granted by **government decree**. For example, when the **British East India Company** was established in 1600, any **competitor** that **breached its trade monopoly** was liable to **forfeiture of their ships and cargo**, as well as **imprisonment** at the "royal pleasure".

NATURAL MONOPOLY

A so-called "**natural monopoly**" occurs when there are **large barriers to entry**, such as the **cost of building infrastructure** or **establishing a network**. An example is a **railway**.

MONOPOLISTIC COMPETITION

A more common situation is **monopolistic competition**, where a **small number of firms divide the market between themselves**. A **key strategy** of the famed investor **Warren Buffett** is to look for companies that have a "**moat**" that **keeps competitors at bay**.

ANTITRUST LEGISLATION

One **role of government** is to **control monopolies**, either through **antitrust legislation** to **break them up**, or in the case of a **natural monopoly** through **price regulations**.

Of course, governments also like to **maintain a few monopolies themselves**, over things like **legal currency**.

MONOPSONY

A monopsony refers to the situation where a market is dominated by a single buyer. The word was coined from the Greek words mónos *for "alone" and* opsōnéō *for "buy provisions", and was popularized by the English economist Joan Robinson in her 1933 book* The Economics of Imperfect Competition.

PRICE MAKER

In a monopsony, the **buyer has the power to set the price** of whatever it is they are buying. A standard example would be a **mining town**, where there is a **single major employer** who can **control the price of labour**.

APPLE VS PEPPER

In 2019, the word became topical in the **Supreme Court case of Apple vs Pepper**. This had nothing to do with the relative merits of fruits or vegetables, but referred to a **class action** headed by **lead plaintiff Robert Pepper**. The accusation was that **Apple** typically takes a 30 per cent **cut on every app sale** that takes place through its **App Store**, which **hurts consumers**.

The court decided that, because Apple is the **sole purchaser of these apps**, it has the **power to set prices**, so could therefore be **sued "on a monopsony theory"**.

Some economists believe that one reason **wage growth** in recent years has been **depressed** is because **companies have increasing monopsony power over their workers**. We might not live in a company town, but **restrictions**, from **geographical constraints** to **non-compete agreements**, **inhibit a worker's ability to get the best wage**.

EXTERNALITIES

Externalities are side effects or consequences of an economic activity that affect other parties but are not reflected in prices, so are another type of market failure.

POSITIVE OR NEGATIVE

An example of a **positive externality** would be an **owner restoring a historic building**, which also helps to **lift the tone of the neighbourhood**. A **negative externality** is something like **pollution**.

THE NETWORK EFFECT

Economists also distinguish between **production and consumption externalities**. An example of the latter is the so-called **network effect**. When a **consumer joins a network**, for example by subscribing to a **phone package**, they **enlarge the network** and **increase its value**.

Externalities can be **analysed** using the **supply and demand figure**, where there are **two supply lines**. The first represents the case when **only private costs are accounted for**, the second higher line is the case when **true social costs are accounted for**. If the **private line** is used, then the **price is too low to cover the true costs**.

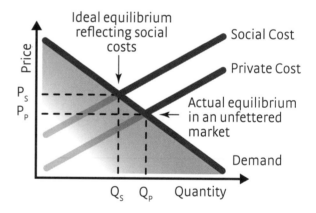

As the British economist **Arthur C. Pigou** pointed out in his 1920 book ***The Economics of Welfare***, **policy-makers** can attempt to **compensate** for **negative externalities** through policies such as **taxing the product**. An example is a **carbon tax**.

A difficulty in practice is that the **true costs of externalities** can only be **estimated indirectly**, and **power structures** mean that they tend to be **underestimated** – one reason for the **climate crisis**.

THE GREAT DEPRESSION

The Great Depression started in the United States with the Wall Street Crash of 1929, and spread in a domino effect through other industrialized countries as international debts were called in.

ECONOMIC COLLAPSE

By 1933, **world GDP** had **decreased** by about 15 per cent, **unemployment** had reached 25 per cent in several countries, and **world trade** had **collapsed** to about a third of its previous value, in part because of **protectionist policies** such as **import tariffs**.

In the **US** alone, around nine thousand **banks** – a third of the total – had collapsed, causing a **monetary contraction** and **deflation**. There was no such thing as **depositor insurance**, so people simply **lost their savings**.

NEW DEAL

After President **Franklin D. Roosevelt** was inaugurated in March 1933, he declared a national "**bank holiday**", where **banks were closed** for a **five-day cooling-off period** to stem the **flood of withdrawals**, famously saying that "**The only thing we have to fear is fear itself.**"

The US soon began to **recover**, with help from Roosevelt's **New Deal programme**, which used **government money** to **stimulate the economy**, but in other countries the **depression lingered** through the 1930s. The resulting **social unrest** helped bring the **Nazi Party** to power in **Germany**.

While economists remain divided over the **causes of the Great Depression**, the event came as a **major shock** to the **relatively new profession**, and paved the way for a **new economic approach** led by **John Maynard Keynes**.

KEYNES

John Maynard Keynes (1883–1946) is generally seen as the most important economist of the first half of the twentieth century.

THE MACRO PICTURE

Keynes represented Britain at the **Versailles Peace Conference** after the **First World War**, and argued that the **peace terms** were **too vindictive** against Germany. His ***The Means to Prosperity*** (1933) was followed by his *magnus opus*, ***The General Theory of Employment, Interest and Money*** (1936).

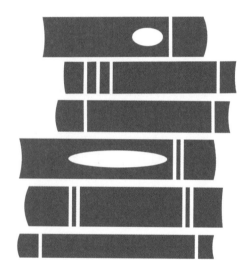

While **neoclassical economists** such as **Alfred Marshall** had focused mostly on **microeconomics**, and saw a **national economy** as a **scaled-up version** of the same thing, Keynes effectively **invented the field** of **modern macroeconomics**.

DEMAND TRAP

According to Keynes – and as illustrated by the **Great Depression**, which was still unfolding at the time – a **national economy** could find itself **stuck in a self-reinforcing equilibrium state** of **low demand** and **high unemployment**.

In **classical theory**, a **decrease in the level of the money supply** M has **no effect** other than to **deflate the price level** P. However, this assumes that prices **instantly adjust**. In reality, **workers resist having their wages lowered**, and **people save money** to **restore their finances**, which **decreases demand**.

GOVERNMENT ACTION

In order to **restore employment**, the **government** therefore **needed to boost the level of demand in the economy**, either by **increasing public spending**, or **cutting taxes**.

TIMELINE

1883 Keynes born in Cambridge, England

1919 Versailles Peace Conference

1933 Published *The Means to Prosperity*

1936 Published *The General Theory of Employment, Interest and Money*

1944 Bretton Woods Conference

1946 Dies

PROPENSITY

Key to Keynesian economics is the idea of our propensity to save or spend.

MARGINAL PROPENSITY

In **classical economics**, people were assumed to **spend** or **invest** any **extra funds**, but this ignored factors such as **uncertainty**. Suppose that a household receives an **extra pound of income**. If they **spend** £0.70, and **save** the remaining £0.30, then their **marginal propensity to consume** is 0.7, and their **marginal propensity to save** is 0.3.

The **marginal propensity differs from** the **average propensity**, since a consumer is **more likely to spend** the **first unit of currency** they receive than they are **the last**. This becomes an issue in a **highly unequal society**, where **rich people tend to save** rather than **spend** or **invest**, which can **slow the economy**.

PARADOX OF THRIFT

In a **recession**, the **propensity to save increases over the whole economy**, which similarly **starves the economy of funds** and **worsens the recession**. Keynes wasn't the first person to recognize this "**paradox of thrift**", but he did give it the catchy name.

Keynes was a **forerunner** of the **behavioural economists** discussed later, in that he believed the **behaviour** of both **consumers** and **investors** was strongly affected by **psychological factors**. For example, it is **easy for workers to accept a rise**, but much **harder to accept a pay cut**, which is why **wages** are **sticky on the way down**.

UNITED KINGDOM HOUSEHOLD SAVING RATIO

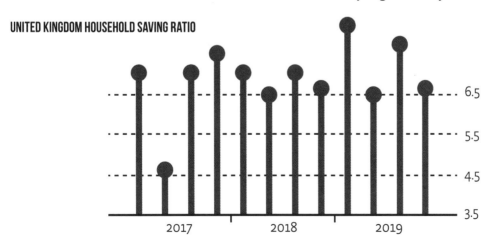

THE MULTIPLIER

According to Keynes, one reason government action is effective is because of the multiplier effect, which scales up the effect of spending.

GOVERNMENT SPENDING

Suppose for example that the **government decides to spend** a certain amount on **infrastructure**. Those people who will **receive the money** will **save a portion** but **spend the rest**, which in turn **lifts the income of other people**. At the **large scale**, this **increases employment**, which in turn makes **people richer**, thus **multiplying the original investment**.

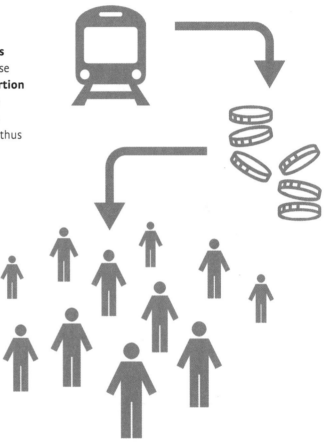

The effect **depends on** the **marginal propensity to consume**. If people **save** half of the money and **spend** the rest, then the **multiplier** is 2, meaning the **initial investment** is effectively **doubled**. In practice, the multiplier is **hard to estimate**, but **Keynes** thought it was about 2.5 in the **United States** at the time.

ANIMAL SPIRITS

Another reason **government action** worked, though, was because of a **different kind of multiplier**, which acted through the effect on the country's **"animal spirits"**. **Investors** have to deal with much **uncertainty** when they make **investment decisions**, and are therefore particularly **susceptible to shifts in sentiment**. The government could therefore **nurse the economy out of a recession** by giving it a boost of an **artificial mood-altering stimulus**.

THE LONG AND THE SHORT TERM

The impact of economic policy depends on the time scale.

SUPPLY CREATES DEMAND

Neoclassical economists believed that, in the **long term**, **supply created its own demand (Say's law)**, since **prices would adjust until markets cleared**. In a **long-term equilibrium** with **full employment**, a **country's output** should be **determined not by demand**, but by factors such as **labour** and **capital**, so should be **independent of price level**. This implied that the **long-run aggregate supply curve** was **vertical**.

DEMAND CREATES SUPPLY

Keynes, however, believed that, at least **in times of recession**, it was **demand that created its own supply (Keynes' Law)**. When the economy is in a recession, a **shift in the demand curve increases output** but has **little effect on price**, because the **supply curve** is **nearly horizontal**. The trick to **boosting the economy** in the **short term** was therefore to **increase aggregate demand**.

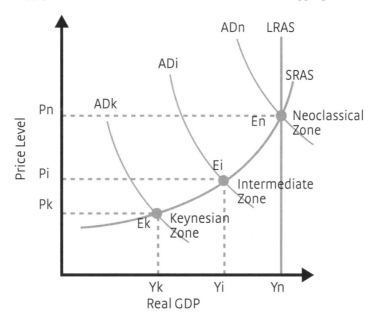

Many economists see **Keynes' Law** as **valid in the short term**, and the **neoclassical view as valid in the long term**. (Sceptics might worry about what happens in the **medium term**.)

In the event of a **demand shock**, such as a **sudden fall in consumer confidence**, **Keynesian cures** can therefore act as a **short-term palliative**, but they are **not a long-term solution**. Though, as Keynes famously said, "**In the long run we are all dead.**"

NEOCLASSICAL SYNTHESIS

Neoclassical economics focused mostly on the micro scale of individual transactions, while Keynes' macroeconomics applied to the scale of the economy as a whole. Following the war, a number of economists therefore began work on joining these theories together.

THE BIG AND THE SMALL

In the same way that **Marshall** summed up **microeconomics** with the **diagram of supply and demand**, so economists came up with **similar diagrams** for the **macro level**. These included the **Phillips curve**, which links **unemployment** and **inflation**, and the **IS-LM curve**, which links **interest rates** and **output**.

NEOCLASSICAL SYNTHESIS

This "**neoclassical synthesis**" was **popularized** by the American economist **Paul Samuelson** (1915–2009), who coined the term. If **Marshall** wrote the **bestselling textbook** for the first half of the twentieth century, **Paul Samuelson's** *Economics* (first published 1948) was the bestseller of the second half, selling over four million copies.

MAXIMIZATION AND EQUILIBRIUM

Samuelson's book aimed to express **core economic theories** in a **consistent mathematical framework**, based on the **related principles** of **maximization** and **equilibrium**. Firms and **individuals act rationally to maximize utility**, and this **drives markets** – and the **economy as a whole** – toward a **stable equilibrium**. Issues such as **imperfect competition** were treated as "**frictions**", which affected this **ideal equilibrium**.

MILTON FRIEDMAN

While the neoclassical synthesis stripped out many of the fuzzier aspects of Keynesian economics, including behavioural effects such as animal spirits, for many economists it was still insufficiently rigorous. Chief among these was Milton Friedman.

 DATE 1912–2006

 NATIONALITY AMERICAN

 SCHOOL CHICAGO SCHOOL

 MAIN WORKS *A THEORY OF THE CONSUMPTION FUNCTION; CAPITALISM AND FREEDOM*

MONETARISM

If **Keynes** was the **most influential economist** of the **first half of the twentieth century**, then **Milton Friedman dominated much of the second**. Friedman derived his intellectual inspiration from Adam Smith and the Austrian economists. A skilled writer and debater, his **main contribution to economic thought** was his work on **monetarism**. According to this theory, **markets are inherently stable**. The **government's job** is to **make sure that the supply of money matches the increase in GDP**. Otherwise, it should **leave the economy alone**, because its **actions** would only **distort markets** and lead to **unintended consequences**.

GDP

STAGFLATION

Friedman's position appeared to be vindicated in the 1970s by the **simultaneous appearance** in **industrialized countries** of **high unemployment** and **high inflation** – aka **stagflation** – which **eluded Keynesian analysis**. In the **US**, the **so-called misery index**, which sums **unemployment** and **inflation**, reached 21 per cent. In the **UK**, it led to the 1978/9 "**winter of discontent**" with **widespread strikes**.

President **Richard Nixon** famously said in 1971, "**We are all Keynesians now**." But when **Ronald Reagan** (in 1981) and **Margaret Thatcher** (in 1979) came to power, their **economic muse** was **not Keynes** but **Friedman**.

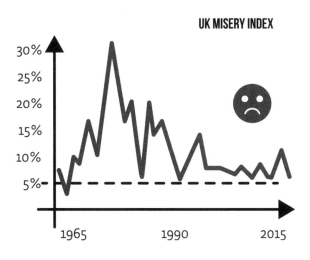

UK MISERY INDEX

30%
25%
20%
15%
10%
5%

1965   1990   2015

THE CHICAGO SCHOOL

Friedman was a leader of the Chicago School of Economics, based at the University of Chicago, which was famous for its free-market ideology and opposition to government regulation.

NOBEL PRIZES

Other members of the Chicago School included **Robert Lucas**, **Gary Becker**, and **Eugene Fama**, all of whom would go on to win the **Nobel Memorial Prize in economics**. In fact the **University of Chicago** has **won more of the prizes than any other university**.

LUCAS CRITIQUE

The "**Lucas critique**" argued that **macroeconomic models** of the **sort developed by Keynes** were based on **parameters** that would be **invalidated** as **expectations changed in response to policy**. **Economic models** should therefore be "**micro-founded**" on the **behaviour of individuals**.

RATIONAL EXPECTATIONS

In **large part because of the Chicago School**, economics came to be **dominated by the paradigm of "rational expectations"**, which states that **participants in the economy act to maximize their long-term utility**, based on their **expectations for the future**. **Government action** to **stimulate** or **manipulate** the **economy** is **counterproductive** because it **distorts economic signals**. For example, **stimulus may raise wages**, but **workers know that it will also cause inflation**, which **cancels out the benefit**.

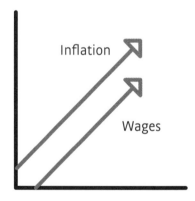

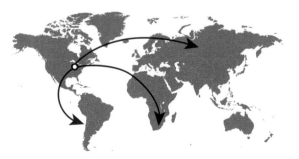

The government should therefore concentrate on the aim of **low inflation** – so **no money printing to stimulate demand** – and policies such as **deregulation** and **trade liberalization**. Versions of this **Chicago model** were rolled out to **countries around the world**, from **Chile** in the 1970s to **South Africa** and **Russia** in the 1990s.

THE MAINSTREAM CONSENSUS

In the late twentieth century, a general consensus emerged among mainstream academic economists.

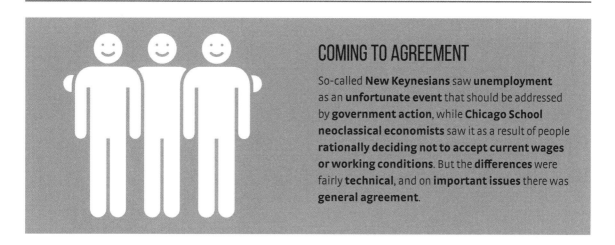

COMING TO AGREEMENT

So-called **New Keynesians** saw **unemployment** as an **unfortunate event** that should be addressed by **government action**, while **Chicago School neoclassical economists** saw it as a result of people **rationally deciding not to accept current wages or working conditions**. But the **differences** were fairly **technical**, and on **important issues** there was **general agreement**.

DEPRESSION PREVENTION

By 2003, Nobel laureate **Robert Lucas** could tell his audience that "My thesis in this lecture is that **macroeconomics** in this **original sense** has **succeeded**: Its central problem of **depression prevention** has been **solved**, for all **practical purposes**, and has in fact been **solved for many decades**."

This turned out to be a little **premature**, since just a few years later the world would find itself in the depths of a **historic crisis**, that in some respects **rivalled the Great Depression**.

KEYNESIAN FRICTIONS

The **mainstream model of the economy** was **neoclassical** with some **Keynesian frictions**. The belief in **rational expectations** and **self-stabilizing economies** shaped **economic policy** from **governments**, **central banks**, and **international organizations**. Economics was viewed as the "**queen of the social sciences**" for its emphasis on **mathematical rigour**.

THE MACROECONOMY

Macroeconomics refers to the study of the economy as a whole, and concerns phenomena such as growth, inflation, and unemployment.

CLASSICAL THEORY

Classical economists tackled the above issues by **dividing the economy into three main markets**. The first was the **product market**, which covers **household consumption**. The second was the **market for the three factors of production** – **land**, **labour**, and **capital**. Finally there was a **market for loanable funds**. Each of these was analysed in terms of **supply** and **demand**.

PRODUCTION

The **product market** represented the **economy's output** – i.e. the **sum total of goods and services consumed** – as a **single product**, whose **supply** depended on things like **capital** and **labour**.

CONSUMPTION

The **consumers demanding this product** were **households**, the **governments**, and the **firms** themselves. **Household consumption** depends on **income**, but because the economy was treated as a **closed loop**, these were **related**: **money spent on consumption (output)** eventually **ends up in people's pockets (income)**.

The economy would **hire workers**, or **borrow funds for investment**, at **rates that corresponded to the marginal return of labour or capital**, and were **subject to a diminishing rate of returns**. The **supply of labour** depended on **wages**, but the **supply of capital** was assumed to be **fixed**. In this **classical picture**, any **extra money** would **always be invested**.

INVESTMENT

In classical economics, investment referred to the production of goods, such as factories and machinery, that can be used in turn to produce other goods.

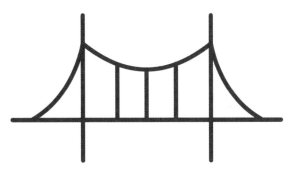

INVESTMENT EQUALS SAVINGS

Classical economists assumed that the **sum total of all investment equalled the total of all savings**. This came from **households**, who **invest their extra cash**, and the **government**. The **incentive to invest** in something like a **factory** was the **expected profit**, **minus costs** such as the **purchase of the building and machinery**, **depreciation**, and so on.

OPEN ECONOMY

In an **open economy**, where **finance is international**, countries are **free to invest in each other**, so this **rule doesn't apply**. Indeed, the term **"investment"** today usually refers to the **speculative purchase** of **financial securities** such as **stocks** and **bonds**.

LONG-TERM GROWTH

Investment is seen as a **trade-off** between **short-term consumption** and **long-term benefit**. The **reason** people and firms **invest** funds, rather than **spend** them, is that they **hope to make more money in the future**. Investment is therefore **key to economic growth**, which is why **governments** often try to **promote it**, either **directly** through **public spending**, or **indirectly** through **tax breaks** or **subsidies**.

Of course this **only works if the money is actually invested in something useful**.

INTEREST RATES

An interest rate is the cost of borrowing money, which depends on both the lender (loan sharks are expensive) and the borrower.

DIFFERENT RATES

When used **generically**, the **interest rate** often refers to the rate that a **central bank charges other banks for short-term loans**. **Bond yields**, which are the **interest paid on bonds**, give a **more accurate picture of longer-term rates**, and are affected by factors such as **inflation**. The **real interest rate** strips out the **effect of inflation**.

DEMAND

A firm's **demand for investment funds** will depend on the **expected earnings** from the investment, **minus the real interest rate**. If the firm **has money already**, then the **real interest rate represents the opportunity cost of not investing it**. (In the **classical model**, firms are anyway assumed to earn **zero economic profit**, so **cannot afford investment without a loan**.)

SUPPLY

The **supply of investment funds** in a **closed economy**, meanwhile, **equals the sum of private and public saving**, which in turn **equals the difference between total output and total spending by consumers and government**.

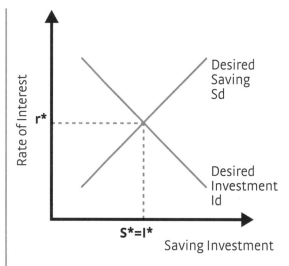

REAL INTEREST RATE

Following the **logic of supply and demand** in **perfectly competitive markets**, classical economists assumed that the **real interest rate** – i.e. the **price of loans** – **adjusts in order to bring the supply of investment funds in balance with demand**.

As we'll see, the reality is **much more complicated**, especially in an **open economy**.

GROSS DOMESTIC PRODUCT (GDP)

The GDP is a measure of a country's national output, and is defined as the total amount spent for all final goods and services produced within a country.

SIMON KUZNETS

The economist **Simon Kuznets** developed the idea of the **gross domestic product** in the 1930s as a way to **determine the impact** of the **Great Depression**. He initially wanted to **exclude** spending on things like **financial speculation**, **advertising**, and **armaments**, on the basis that they **did not contribute to human well-being**. However, **GDP** was adopted by **US planners** during the **Second World War** as a **way to track military spending**, and during the **Cold War** it was used as a kind of **proxy indicator** for **economic supremacy**.

CALCULATION

GDP can be **calculated in three ways**. The **production approach** adds up the **value of all final goods and services** (as opposed to **intermediaries** that **make up the final product**). The **income method** adds the **income of all producers**, including **people** and **firms**. The **expenditures method** adds up all **spending on final goods**.

The **formula for aggregate expenditure** is Y = C + I + G + X − M, where:
C = consumption
I = investment in new capital goods or inventory
G = government expenditure
X = exports sold
M = imports purchased

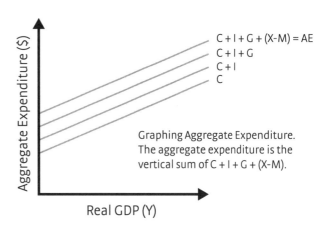

Graphing Aggregate Expenditure. The aggregate expenditure is the vertical sum of C + I + G + (X-M).

In theory, the **three methods should agree**, since **earnings are spent on goods that are produced**. In practice, measurement is a **complex procedure**, so each method gives a **slightly different picture**.

CONSUMPTION

In most industrialized countries, by far the most important component of GDP is consumption.

TOTAL SPEND

In the **US**, for example, consumption currently constitutes about **70 per cent of GDP**, with **investment** and **government spending** making up the rest in about **equal proportion**, and **net exports** representing a **small loss**.

Since **what one person spends** is **what another person earns**, **total consumption** C equals **total income** Y. If the **average income tax rate** is T, then the **disposable income**, defined as what is **left over after tax**, is $Y_D = Y(1-T)$.

In the **Keynesian model**, a person's **rate of consumption** depends on their **marginal propensity to consume**, which is denoted c. The formula is then

$$C = C_0 + cY_D = C_0 + cY(1-T)$$

where C_0 is the **baseline amount** that is needed for **everyday life** (and can be **borrowed if necessary**).

Plugging the **formula for C** into the **formula for aggregate expenditure used in the GDP calculation** gives

$$Y = C_0 + cY(1-T) + I + G + X - M$$

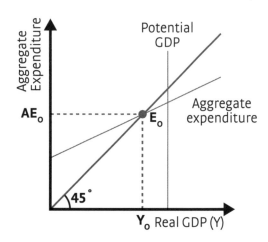

MULTIPLIER

The **equilibrium point**, where the **two sides are equal**, can be found by **plotting the right-hand side against a 45-degree line**. The graph illustrates the **multiplier effect**, because a **vertical shift in aggregate expenditure** induced by **government spending** G results in a **horizontal shift in GDP** by an **amount greater than G** – **money for nothing** and your **growth for free**! At least, until you hit an **environmental tipping point**.

GROWTH FACTORS

While much of classical economics focuses on the concept of equilibrium, classical economists were of course very aware of the explosive rate of economic growth that characterized the Industrial Revolution.

FACTORS OF PRODUCTION

The **size of the economy** in **Western Europe tripled** in **real terms** over the course of the **nineteenth century**. **Classical economists** saw such **growth** as being **caused by increases in the factors of production**, which were **land**, **labour**, and **capital**.

One way to create **economic growth** was to **cultivate new land**, as **settlers** at the time were doing in the **United States**.

Another way was to **increase the amount of labour** – either through **population growth**, or by making the **existing labour force more efficient**.

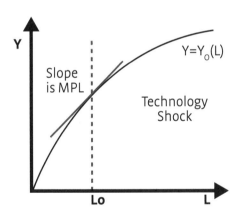

The third method was to use **capital**, which refers to the **non-human assets** such as **machines**, **buildings**, **stocks of materials**, and so on. Or, as **Adam Smith** put it, "**That part of a man's stock which he expects to afford him revenue is called his capital**."

CLASS ANALYSIS

In **classical economics**, each **factor of production** was associated with a **distinct class**: the **landowners**, the **labourers**, and the **capitalists**. While classical economists assumed any **savings** would be **immediately invested in real assets**, **today** any **analysis of capital** has to include **financial assets** such as **cash**, **bonds**, or **stocks**.

DIVISION OF LABOUR

Adam Smith believed that a main cause of economic growth at the time was increasing division of labour.

PIN FACTORY

Smith illustrated this through his famous example of a **pin factory employing ten workers**, each of whom has a **separate task**.

"One man **draws out the wire**, another **straights it**, a third **cuts it**, a fourth **points it**, a fifth **grinds it** at the top for receiving a head; to **make the head** requires **two or three distinct operations**; to **put it on**, is a peculiar business, to **whiten the pins** is another ... The important business of **making a pin** is, in this manner, **divided into about eighteen distinct operations**."

In this way the factory could produce **48,000 pins in a day**, which averages to **4,800 per worker**. But Smith estimated that **one person working independently** could only produce about **twenty pins a day**.

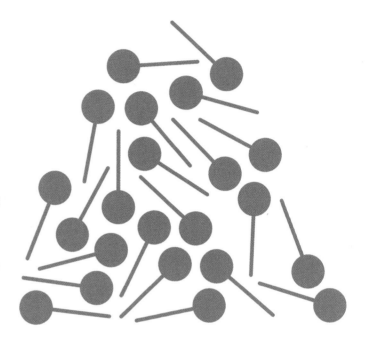

TECHNOLOGY

It is certainly true that **specialization** boosts **productivity**, especially for **complex products**. However, as a number of commentators have pointed out, Smith's **optimistic analysis** does not seem a realistic description of **actual pin-making factories** of the time, and ignores the **more powerful factor**, which is **technology**. A **machine** could produce **even more pins** all by itself, which highlights the **tension between workers and capitalists** that concerned **Marx**.

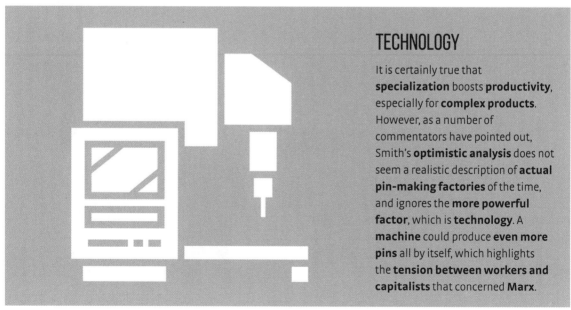

COMPARATIVE ADVANTAGE

The theory of comparative advantage was proposed by the English economist David Ricardo (1772–1823).

SPECIALIZATION

Ricardo illustrated the theory using a **simple example** of two countries, **Portugal** and **England**, **trading two products**, **wine** and **cloth**. He demonstrated that each country would **benefit** if it **concentrated only on manufacturing whichever good it could produce more cheaply**, and **importing the other**. "In fact," he claimed, "it is **difficult to say where the limit is** at which you would cease to **accumulate wealth**."

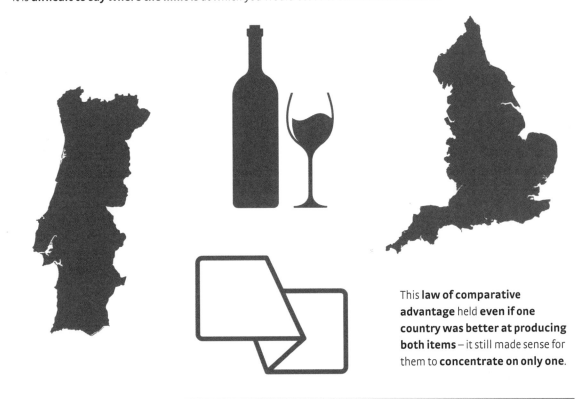

This **law of comparative advantage** held **even if one country was better at producing both items** – it still made sense for them to **concentrate on only one**.

FREE TRADE

The **monopolies, tariffs, guilds**, and **government interference** that characterized **mercantilism** might appear on the surface to **promote economic growth**, but in fact they **retarded it**. And **just as workers should specialize, so should nations**.

Ricardo's simplified analysis **ignored many complicating factors**, such as the fact that **workers or factories cannot easily switch what they produce**. However, the proof of his theory inspired many with its application of **deductive logic**. The economist **Paul Samuelson** even described it as the **only proposition in social science** that "is **both true and non-trivial**".

THOMAS MALTHUS

While classical economists held a generally optimistic view of economic growth, Ricardo's friend, the curate and scholar Thomas Malthus (1766–1834), pointed out a potentially huge problem, which was that population grows even faster.

GEOMETRIC VERSUS ARITHMETIC

Malthus' argument was that **population increases** in a **geometric fashion** (i.e. 2, 4, 8, 16, 32...) while subsistence grows in an arithmetic fashion (2, 4, 6, 8, 10...) and the **former will always win.**

NATURAL SELECTION

In light of his observations, Malthus **opposed measures** to **alleviate poverty**, since they would only **encourage the poor to have more children**. His theory was a **key influence** for **Charles Darwin's theory of natural selection. Technological progress**, and the **inverse relation** between **wealth** and **fertility**, have, so far at least, **postponed the day of reckoning.**

EXPLODING POPULATION

To back up his argument, **Malthus** drew on research by the American scientist **Benjamin Franklin** showing that the **American population tended to double every twenty-five years** (although this **included immigration**). However, his **worries about population growth** were also shaped by the **Industrial Revolution**, where the **influx** of people to **urban centres** such as **London** was **making poverty very visible**.

As Malthus painted it, the **collision between population growth and natural limits wouldn't end well**: "**Sickly seasons, epidemics, pestilence**, and **plague**, advance in terrific array, and sweep off their thousands and ten thousands. Should success be still incomplete, gigantic inevitable **famine** stalks in the rear, and with **one mighty blow levels the population**."

THE STEADY-STATE ECONOMY

The classical picture of macroeconomics emphasized a steady state. Like a tree, the economy grows to a certain height, and then stays there.

UNEMPLOYMENT

When applied to **labour**, the **law of supply and demand** implied that the **price of labour will adjust to meet the level of demand**. There will therefore be **no involuntary unemployment**. Anyone who **wants work can get it**, just by **lowering their asking wage**.

THE ART OF LIVING

Finally, while **classical economists** did study **economic growth**, they saw it as a **temporary process**. As **John Stuart Mill** noted, "the **increase of wealth is not boundless**" and **diminishing returns** would mean that the **economy would eventually settle** into what he called a "**stationary state**". He saw this as a **positive** thing, since it would allow people to focus on "**the Art of Living**" instead of "**the Art of Getting On**".

SAY'S LAW

For similar reasons there can be no such thing as a **general glut**, where there is a widespread **excess of supply over demand**. According to **Say's law**, named after the French economist **Jean-Baptiste Say** (1767–1832), "**supply creates its own demand**". The **money spent on the production of a good** is used to buy something else. At the **macro scale**, **doubling production** therefore **doubles income**, which **doubles consumption**.

In this analysis, there weren't any **savings**, because **any available money** would be **invested in real assets** such as **machines**. In fact **money didn't play any role at all**, other than as an **inert means of exchange**.

MONETARY POLICY

Central banks use monetary policy to control the money supply in the hope of managing demand. Conventional policy tools include adjustments to short-term interest rates, and open-market operations.

MACROECONOMICS

DISCOUNT RATE

The discount rate is the **rate that the central bank charges other banks** for the **short-term loans** that they need to **top up reserves. Lowering the discount interest rate frees up cash**, which **commercial banks can loan**, which has the effect of **lowering interest rates** and – at least in principle – **boosting demand** in the **wider economy**.

OPEN-MARKET OPERATIONS

Open-market operations are where the **central bank buys or sells financial securities** such as **government or company bonds**. If, for example, the aim is to **boost the economy**, the central bank can **buy those securities from commercial banks**. This **increases the amount of cash held by those banks**, and **adds to the money supply**.

An **increase in the supply of money** tends to **decrease the**

price charged for it, as **reflected by interest rates**. The **net effect** is therefore to **lower the interest rate at which commercial banks lend to one another**.

Central banks sometimes also **buy or sell the securities of other countries** in order to **influence the exchange rate**. This is one reason the **Bank of China** currently holds over a **trillion dollars' worth of US government debt**.

BONDS

A bond is a financial security that promises future payments in return for the purchase price.

TERMINOLOGY

The **face value** of a **bond** is the **amount paid on maturity**, while **coupon payments** represent the **regular interest payments** (so named because in pre-computer days people would tear a coupon off the bottom of the bond and mail it in for payment).

YIELD

The bond's **initial yield** is the **income earned** from a bond, **divided by the price**. The **total yield**, however, **depends on the price**, which is **set by the market as the bond is traded**. For example, if you buy a **zero-coupon one-year £1,000 bond for just £950**, then even though the **interest is zero**, you still make a **return of about 5 per cent** when you **cash it in**. In general, **bond prices vary inversely with interest rates**, so **higher interest rates lead to lower bond prices** and **vice versa**.

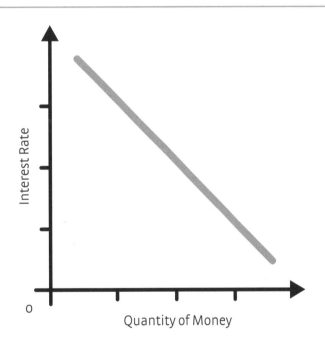

INTEREST RATES

The **bond market** acts as a **corrective force** on **interest rates**. If, say, the **interest rate** is **too low**, then the **demand for money**, or **liquidity preference**, will be **high** (since the **opportunity cost of holding cash** is **low**). People will therefore **sell bonds in exchange for money**, which **lowers their price**, which leads to **higher interest rates**.

YIELD CURVE

Yields also vary with the time until maturity. The yield curve is a plot of the interest rate on government bonds, as a function of the maturity time. Economists and investors alike closely watch the yield curve, on the belief that it acts as a portent of market sentiment.

SLOPE

The **slope of the yield curve** gives a sense of **how investors think interest rates and market risk will change over time**. Normally the yield curve **slopes upward**, because **investors want higher interest** to **compensate for the risk of locking up their funds for a long time**.

INVERSION

If the curve **slopes downward**, this is a **signal** that **investors** are **anticipating** that **interest rates may be lower in the future**. Such a "**yield rate inversion**" is often considered a **harbinger of recession**.

SHIFTS

When the **whole yield curve moves up**, this means that investors are **anticipating higher inflation**, so need **higher interest**. When it **drops**, it implies that investors are **sanguine about the prospects of inflation**; or that other **asset classes are unappealing**, so investors are **crowding into bonds**.

Yields can also be **compared** between **different bond types**. The yield demanded by investors **depends on the risk of the lender defaulting on the bond**. A **government bond pays the lowest interest**, while **junk bonds pay a higher yield** but might also **pay nothing if the company goes bust**.

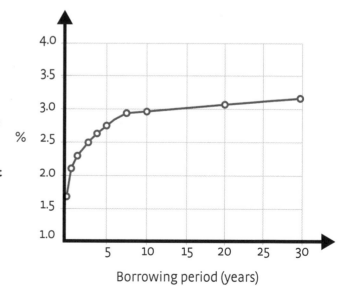

Borrowing period (years)

CREDIT RATING

Anyone who has applied for a loan will be familiar with the idea of a credit score, which ranks creditworthiness based on things like existing debts and payment history. Business and governments also get their own version of a credit score, which affects their ability to raise funds.

RATING AGENCIES

The three **main credit rating agencies for business and government** are Moody's **Investors Service**, **Standard & Poor's**, and **Fitch Ratings**.

SCORE CARD

Taking **Moody's** as an example, their **ratings start at Aaa** for "The **highest quality and lowest credit risk**" and "**Best ability to repay short-term debt**". Going down, there are various other **sub-grades of A** (Aa1, Aa2, etc.) until you get to the **Bs**, which are **higher risk**. Anything below Ba is "**junk**". The **bottom grade is C**, which is "Rated as the **lowest quality**, usually in **default** and **low likelihood of recovering principal or interest**."

SOVEREIGN CREDIT RATINGS

Governments put great stake in their **sovereign credit rating**, and for good reason. In 2011, President **Nicolas Sarkozy** was reported to have said that "if France loses its **triple A rating**, I'm dead". It did, and **within a few months** he was **out of office**.

In 1993 **James Carville**, an advisor to President **Bill Clinton**, joked that should he be reincarnated, he would want to come back as the **bond market**, on the basis that "You can **intimidate everyone**." But maybe it would be better to come back as a **ratings agency**.

DEBT

Debt is a fundamental aspect of economic life, if only because the money that we use is based on debt – so if the government repaid all its debts, the money would vanish.

GROWTH

Debt is **essential to economic growth**, because **entrepreneurs** (or **regular firms**) usually need to **borrow money** in order to **pursue their crazy dreams**. And it is pretty hard for most people to **buy a house** in a major city without taking on a mind-blowing **mortgage**.

GLOBAL DEBT

In recent years, **global debt levels** – including **sovereign and corporate loans** – have exploded to almost **$250 billion** at the time of writing.

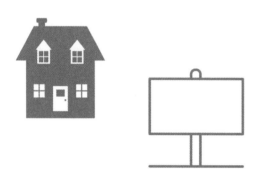

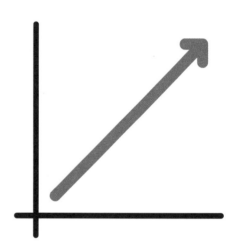

IS DEBT DANGEROUS?

Mainstream economists are **largely sanguine about this development**, because they are accustomed to **modelling the economy using single representational agents**. From this perspective, **debt cancels out in aggregate**, so is **only a problem if it crowds out investment**. Or, as the economist and *New York Times* columnist **Paul Krugman** insisted in 2019: "**DEBT IS MONEY WE OWE TO OURSELVES.**"

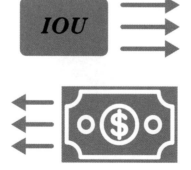

As discussed later, there is a growing realization that this **traditional position ignores** things like the **power difference between debtors and creditors**, the fact that **interest rates are very different for the rich than for the poor**, and the **inherent risks to financial stability**. (In any case, using the same logic, **theft** isn't a problem either, because at the **aggregate level it is money we take from ourselves**.)

TAXES

Tax is from the Latin taxare *meaning "to censure, charge, or compute". It is now so established that there is even a time of year (the tax season) named after it.*

TAXES AND MONEY

Taxes are usually seen as a **kind of charge for government services**, but they are also an **integral part of the money system**. When **coin money** was **first invented** in **Ancient Greece**, taxes were a **way to pay the troops**, but also a **way to ensure the troops were kept supplied** (**suppliers** needed the **soldiers' money** to **pay the taxes**). The Roman emperor **Julius Caesar** was the **first to introduce a general 1 per cent sales tax**, which would have confused the cash registers of the time.

INCOME TAX

In **medieval times**, under the **feudal system**, taxes were usually **paid in kind** or **through labour**, rather than **in cash**, but this **changed** as **money took on a growing role in society**. **Income tax**, which requires detailed knowledge of **how much everyone earns**, is a **relatively modern** phenomenon and **only came into its own during the second half of the twentieth century**, when it was tapped for big-ticket items like **defence spending** and **welfare systems**.

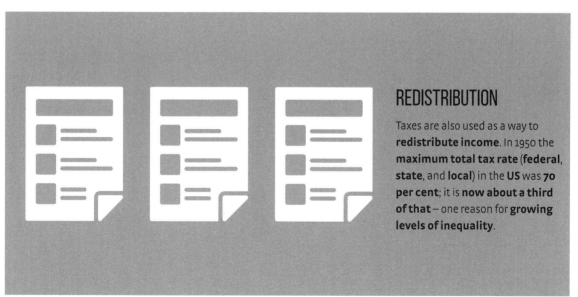

REDISTRIBUTION

Taxes are also used as a way to **redistribute income**. In 1950 the **maximum total tax rate (federal, state**, and **local)** in the **US** was **70 per cent**; it is **now about a third of that** – one reason for **growing levels of inequality**.

THE ECONOMICS OF DEATH

It's an old saying that nothing is as certain as death and taxes. As befitting "the dismal science" moniker, economists also spend quite a lot of time thinking about death.

PRICE OF A LIFE

One question that comes up is, **what is the economic value of saving a life?** Economists estimate this by **computing the marginal cost of death prevention** – for example, **how much money** would **need to be spent** on **upgrading traffic systems** to **reduce the expected number of fatalities by one**.

ANNUITIES

A different type of question is **how long an individual person is expected to live**. For example, an **annuity is a financial instrument** that, in return for an **initial fee**, gives **regular payments until death**. Its **price** therefore **depends on life expectancy**.

MORTGAGES

The literal meaning of the word **"mortgage"** is **"death-pledge"** or **"death grip"**, although mortgages are not marketed this way.

CREDIT DEFAULT

Many of the **mathematical tools** used to **estimate the probability of credit default** have their **roots in models of life expectancy**. For example, **actuaries** have long known that **when one person in a couple dies**, the **chance of the other person dying rises markedly in the next few months**. Mathematical **models** used to **simulate** this **"broken heart syndrome"** were **later adapted to model correlations between mortgage defaults**. The **failure of these models** during the **US mortgage crisis** caused a different kind of heartbreak.

PRICE INDEX

A price index is a statistic that tracks how prices of some items change over time.

CPI

The **consumer price index** (CPI) calculates the **relative price**, normalized to a **base year**, for a **basket of goods** that is supposed to represent **typical spending**. In the **UK**, the basket includes about **seven hundred** items, varying from a **pint at the local pub**, to a **new car**, to a **holiday in the sun**.

Calculating the index is **complicated by a number of factors**. One is that there is **no such thing as an average consumer**, so one person's inflation may be **very different** from another's.

MOVING TARGET

Another problem is that the **market basket changes over time**, as **technology improves**, or as **consumer choices change**. This makes **comparison** across time periods more **difficult**. For example, if an item **becomes very expensive**, then people may **buy less of it**, so it gets a **smaller weight in the basket** and **contributes less to inflation**.

Finally, the cost of the basket **doesn't account for changes in quality of the goods** (e.g. smart phones).

Inflation indices are important not just to **track the economy**, but also because they **determine the prices** of many things, including **pay rises**, **pensions**, and certain **inflation-linked government bonds**.

MARKET INDEX

Indices exist for many things, from **house prices** to **stock markets**. The **Dow Jones Industrial Index**, for example, started in 1896 as the **average price of twelve stocks (later expanded** to thirty) and continues to serve as a **barometer** for the **US stock market**.

NEGATIVE INTEREST RATES

In late 2008, the then US Fed chairman Ben Bernanke introduced an unconventional policy, which was to drop interest rates down to 0 per cent, in order to stimulate lending. In real (after inflation) terms, the interest rate was negative.

GOING NEGATIVE

Bernanke's move started something of a trend, and **negative real interest rates** are now **commonplace**, which suggests that not **all is well with the world economy**. **Central banks** in **Europe** and **Japan** have even experimented with **negative nominal rates**. The **kickstart** has become a **crutch**.

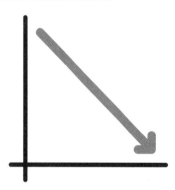

This is obviously good for **debtors**, but less so for **banks**, because the **whole point of banking** is that you **lend out money to make interest**. They can **mitigate the effect** by **charging more in fees**, but **negative interest** still **upends the basic business model**.

ECONOMIC MODELS

Negative interest is also confusing for **economic modellers**. A **key parameter** in **financial models** is the **risk-free interest rate**. If this is negative, then the models give **meaningless results** – they just tell you to **borrow an infinite amount of money**.

Models used to value things like **pensions** rely on a **discount rate**, which plays a **similar role**. If the discount rate is **negative**, any pension would technically be **underfunded**.

WHY?

So why would anyone buy a **bond** with a **negative interest rate**? Either because they are **institutions**, such as **pension funds**, which **have to keep some money in guaranteed bonds**, or they are expecting **deflation**, or they **hope to sell** it **at a profit in the future**, when interest rates are even **lower**.

FISCAL POLICY

Along with monetary policy, another tool the government uses to influence economic activity is fiscal policy.

FIGHTING RECESSIONS

If the government is in **recession-fighting mode**, it can either **reduce taxation** so that individuals have **more money to spend**, or it can **put more money into the economy directly**, by engaging in things like **public works programmes**.

BALANCE THE BUDGET

The aim of such **fiscal measures** is to **reduce unemployment** and **boost demand without triggering inflation**. To **finance** them, the **government** can either **print more money** (generally frowned upon as it may cause **inflation**), or **borrow more money** (very popular because it means **deferring the problem**). The question of **balancing the budget** is a heated **topic of debate** among economists, with supporters of **Modern Monetary Theory** saying that the **state can borrow as much as it pleases** so long as **inflation doesn't become an issue**.

UNEMPLOYMENT INSURANCE

Unemployment insurance acts as an **automatic stabilizer**, because it **ramps up payments** when **unemployment is high**.

GOVERNMENT SIZE

Another question is **how large the government should be in the first place**, **relative to the rest of the economy**. **Government spending** tends to be **higher in European countries**, with **France** and **Finland** leading the way at about 55 per cent of GDP, while in the **UK** it is about 42 per cent, and in the **US** 38 per cent. But you do **get what you pay for**.

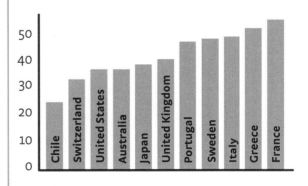

NEOLIBERALISM

The meaning of the word "neoliberalism" is contested – and socialists often use it as a catch-all insult against capitalists – but in economics it is usually associated with the free market ideology of economists such as Milton Friedman.

A NEW FAITH

In his 1951 paper "**Neoliberalism and Its Prospects**", **Friedman** argued that the **laissez-faire liberalism** of the nineteenth century went too far because it **did not assign a meaningful role to the state**. However, the **"collectivist" reaction** that he saw taking place in countries including the **United States** went **too far in the other direction**.

"A **new faith** must avoid both errors. It must give high place to a s**evere limitation on the power of the state** to interfere in the detailed activities of individuals; at the same time, it must **explicitly recognize** that there are **important positive functions** that must be **performed by the state**. The doctrine sometimes called **neo-liberalism** … is such a faith."

Milton Friedman

MONT PELERIN SOCIETY

The "**new faith**" was promoted by the **Mont Pelerin Society**, which **Friedman** helped found in 1947, along with other future Nobel laureates **Friedrich Hayek** and **George Stigler**. It was influential on politicians including **Ronald Reagan** and **Margaret Thatcher**, who at one **Conservative Party** meeting held up a copy of **Hayek's neoliberalist tome,** *The Constitution of Liberty* (1960), and announced: "This is what we believe."

With the current **backlash against neoliberal policies** such as **deregulation** and **hyper-globalization**, economists are increasingly looking for what one 2019 article by three economists called "**new thinking beyond neoliberalism**" (neo-neoliberalism?).

INTERNATIONAL TRADE

International trade is as old as the concept of a nation; however, its volume has ebbed and flowed over time.

OPEN FOR TRADE

For example, international trade grew quickly in the **nineteenth** and **twentieth centuries**; was disrupted by the **First World War**, the **Great Depression**, and the **Second World War**; resumed growth in the **1950s**; slowed in the **1970s** due to the **oil crisis**; and picked up steam again until the **Great Financial Crisis** of 2007/8.

WORLD TRADE

Today, the two most traded items are **oil**, followed closely by **cars** – which explains succinctly why oil is so **key to the world economy**.

TRADE POLICY

Trade policy has always been a **contentious and politically charged** subject. Economists sometimes argue, for example, that if a country holds a **comparative advantage** in cars but not in agriculture, it should concentrate on the former. Yet **Japan** still prefers to produce its own **rice**, even though it **costs Japanese consumers** as much as **ten times more than global prices**.

One reason is that Japanese farmers have a **lot at stake** and are a **powerful lobby**. Another is that countries like to have **control over their food supply**.

The **COVID-19 crisis** drew attention to the fact that many countries are **very reliant on imports** (mostly from China) for **drugs and other critical medical supplies**.

THEORIES OF TRADE

Theories to explain trade patterns include **Ricardo's theory of comparative advantage**, and **New Trade Theory**, which points out the **advantages gained** from **economies of scale** when a country can **enlarge the market** for its goods.

BILATERAL BALANCES

A bilateral trade balance is the difference between how much one country exports to another, and how much it imports.

REASONS TO BE IN DEFICIT

A **positive balance of trade** is often interpreted as **proof** that a country is "**winning**" in the **trade relationship**, as in **mercantilism**, but the **truth is more complicated**.

One reason a country might run a **large trade deficit** is that its firms are **not competitive internationally**, so it is **cheaper to import goods**. In theory, **one remedy** is for the country's **currency to depreciate** until it is **competitive**; a better one is for the country to **improve its firms**.

However, a **negative trade balance** could also be a **sign** that the country is **growing** and **attracting foreign investment**, which **boosts consumption** of things including **foreign goods**. The situation is a bit like having a **negative trade balance** with your **local grocery store** – in either case, you are **getting something in return**.

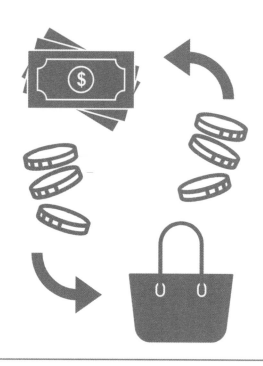

TRADE AGREEMENTS

Countries often negotiate **trade agreements** with **one other country** (**bilateral agreements**), with their **neighbours** (**regional**), or with a **number of countries** (**multilateral**), which **reduce or eliminate trade barriers** such as **tariffs** or **quotas**. The **General Agreement on Tariffs and Trade** (GATT) was established in 1947, and its successor the **World Trade Organization** (WTO) was established in 1995.

However, the **interest in free trade has waned** somewhat since the **Great Financial Crisis**, when its **drawbacks** – such as the **loss of industries to foreign competitors** – became more obvious.

DEVELOPMENT ECONOMICS

Development economics is a branch of economics that applies economic theories to low-income countries.

MERCANTILISM

Perhaps the **first development economists** were the **colonial-era European mercantilists**. However, their aim was **not so much to help developing countries** as to **find ways to exploit their resources better**, in terms of **raw materials** and **human labour** (i.e. slaves). Beginning with the **Industrial Revolution**, the related doctrine of **economic nationalism** meant that **industries in fast-growing countries like the United States** were **protected** through **tariffs** and **subsidies**.

LINEAR GROWTH

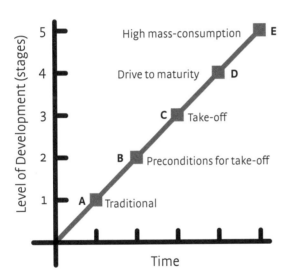

After the **Second World War**, the **"linear stages of growth model"** was developed by economist **W.W. Rostow** in his 1960 book ***The Stages of Growth: A Non-Communist Manifesto***. This posited that countries progress through **five stages**: "the **traditional society**, the **pre-conditions for take-off**, the **take-off**, the **drive to maturity**, and the **age of high mass-consumption**". The **main requirement for growth** was **sufficient capital**, coupled with a **strong public sector** to help **manage it**.

NONLINEAR GROWTH

The model was inspired in part by the success of the **US Marshall Plan** in helping to **rebuild a war-shattered Europe**. However, it **worked less well** when **applied to poor countries** around the world, in part because **capital plus government** is a **formula for corruption**, but also because **development is not a straight line** (*see* Complexity Economics below).

Today, **development economists** tend to concentrate on **more empirical methods**, such as **randomized control trials**.

RANDOMIZED CONTROL TRIALS

In medicine, a randomized controlled trial (RCT) compares outcomes for patients who receive different treatments with a control trial, which could be a standard treatment, a placebo, or no treatment at all. In recent decades, the approach has been applied to other areas as well, including economics.

FIGHTING POVERTY

The 2019 **Nobel** Memorial Prize in Economics was awarded to the team of **Michael Kremer**, **Abhijit Banerjee**, and **Esther Duflo** for their work using **RCTs** to find out **which interventions** are **most effective at combating poverty in developing countries**. For example, a 1990s experiment in **rural Kenya** found that **handing out free textbooks and meals in schools did not improve educational outcomes**. However, other experiments in **India** showed that **tutoring special-needs children did make a difference**.

An experiment by the same team showed that **parents in low-income countries** are **more likely to give their children deworming pills** if those pills are **free**, as opposed to being **heavily subsidized**.

RANDOMISTAS

The **"randomistas"**, as followers of the RCT approach are known, have helped introduce the phrase **"evidence based"** into economics, which is a good thing for a field that is often criticized as being **overly abstract and mathematical**. At the same time, RCTs are **no panacea**. In medicine they are used to get **final regulatory approval for drugs**, but **finding cures for cancer** – or **overcoming the structural problems that underlie world poverty** – will certainly require **more radical thinking**.

PRIVATE PROPERTY

The concepts of private property and ownership rights long predate economics.

HOME OWNERSHIP

Aristotle argued in his ***Politics*** that **private ownership** promotes virtues like **responsibility** and **prudence** (today, people say the same of **home ownership**). Much of **Roman law** was devoted to **defining and protecting ownership**, though there it applied as much to **slaves** as to things like **land**.

DIGITAL PROPERTY

In the **digital age**, **property rights** often refer to **intellectual property** (IP) as much as to the physical kind. The fact that **information can be copied and distributed for free** means that IP can only be **partially protected through patents**.

JOHN LOCKE

In his ***Two Treatises on Government*** (1689), the philosopher **John Locke** argued that the **main function of the state** was to **protect the rights and freedoms of its citizens**. This included **property rights**, which he believed are generated when people **mix their labour with the material world**.

For example, an **apple on a tree** is of **no use** to a person, but when they **pick it**, they **add their labour to it** and therefore **transform it into a valuable object**: as Locke wrote, "His labour hath taken it out of the hands of nature … and hath thereby **appropriated it to himself**." **Money** was a way of both **crystallizing these gains**, and of **asserting and guaranteeing one's freedom**.

Locke's work provided **political and philosophical justification** for the **accumulation of money and property**, and also served as **one of the main influences** on the **constitution of the new American government** in 1787.

THE COMMONS

Apart from private property (capitalism) and collective property (communism), a third option is common ownership.

ENCLOSURE

Under the **feudal system** in **Europe**, for example, large areas were **reserved** as **collectively managed commons** that were used for purposes such as **animal grazing** and **collecting firewood**. As the feudal system **broke down**, **tenants** were increasingly **evicted from common land** as part of a **privatization process**. In **England** this "enclosure" began in the **thirteenth century** and was **still in progress** when **Locke** was writing his **theory of property rights**.

ELINOR OSTROM

While **Hardin's parable** was very **influential** among economists, **empirical evidence** shows that people **can manage commons areas** – including **forests, fisheries, irrigation systems, grasslands**, and so on – very **successfully**, with **no help from economic experts**. The political scientist **Elinor Ostrom** won her economics **Nobel** for her work in this area.

TRAGEDY OF THE COMMONS

The **idea of the commons** seems **incompatible** with **traditional economics**, for reasons captured in a 1968 paper called "**The Tragedy of the Commons**" from ecologist **Garrett Hardin**. This described a number of **animal herders** who all have **access to an area of common pasture**. For each herder, **self-interest** dictates that they should **exploit the land** as much as possible; but if they all do this, the result is **over-grazing**, and the land becomes **unproductive for all**.

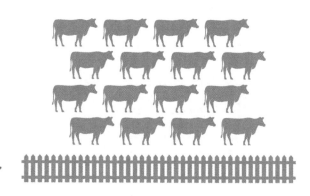

MARKETS

Like property rights, markets have been around much longer than the discipline of economics, and have social dimensions that are not obviously apparent in a purely economic treatment.

INSTITUTIONS

The economist **Karl Polanyi** (1886–1964) argued that **markets** are **best viewed** as "**embedded** and **enmeshed** in **institutions**, **economic** and **noneconomic**". As he stated many times: "**market economy** is an **institutional structure**".

These **institutions** include a system of **property rights** and **contract law**; **financial services** such as **credit**; **public infrastructure** such as **power** and **transportation**; access to a **reliable and educated workforce**; a **secure environment** protected by **public policing**; a **system for informing consumers**; and so on.

SOCIAL NORMS

Markets are also influenced by **social norms**. **Polanyi's theory** was inspired in part by **anthropological studies** of **non-industrialized societies**. A **behaviour** that might seem **reasonable** from a **rational utility-maximizing standpoint** will look **very different** in a **traditional gift-giving society** where **land**, **labour**, and **money** are **not treated as profit-making commodities**.

Following the **Great Financial Crisis**, **anthropologists** such as **Joris Luyendijk** increasingly turned their attention to the strange and isolated tribe known as **financial traders**, who worshipped a god called "**the bonus**".

MONEY

In particular, **money-based markets** rely on the **existence** and **maintenance** of a **stable currency**. As seen in the section on money, the **money system didn't come from nowhere**, but is best viewed as a **carefully designed** and **maintained piece** of **social technology**.

FREE MARKET ECONOMY

A free market economy is one that promotes the basic tenets of economic freedom.

INDIVIDUAL FREEDOM

The **tenets of economic freedom** include **private ownership of property**, a **lack of price regulation**, **minimal restrictions by the government**, and a system that, as **Milton Friedman** put it in 1984, "takes the **individual** – or the **family**, if you will – as the **key element in society**. I would like to see a society in which individuals have the **maximum freedom** to **pursue their own objectives** in **whichever direction they wish**, so long as they **don't interfere with the rights of others to do the same thing**."

ECONOMIC FREEDOM

The concept of economic freedom is also **hard to pin down**, because **one person's freedom is often another person's servitude**. According to the **Heritage Foundation**, the **world's most economically free county** at the time of writing is **Hong Kong**, and the **leader in Latin America** is **Chile**. Both of these countries have recently been affected by **massive protests**, fuelled in part by long-standing **frustration over economic issues** such as **inequality**.

UTOPIA

In a **free market**, **prices** are **set** by the "**law of supply and demand**" with **no interference** from the **state**. It therefore implicitly assumes that **markets** are **competitive**, **people act rationally** to **optimize their own utility**, and that **all players have access to perfect information**. Of course, **no real society meets these standards** (**Friedman** was describing a "**personal utopia**").

COMMUNISM

The word communism is from the Latin communis, *for "common" or "universal", and a communist state aims to erase economic distinctions between people based on things like power and class.*

MARXIST ECONOMICS

At **Karl Marx**'s sparsely attended **London funeral** in 1883, his friend and admirer **Engels** said, "His name and work will **endure** through the ages." Even Engels might have been surprised though to know that by the mid-point of the next century, **about a third of the world would describe itself as run by Marxist ideas**.

CENTRALIZATION

Marx put it like this: **"From each according to his ability, to each according to his needs."** Of course, someone has to decide on **what those abilities and needs are**, and under **communism** this is **not Smith's invisible hand**, but the **visible hand of the state**. As **Nikita Khrushchev**, who was Stalin's successor as leader of the **Soviet Union**, wrote in his memoirs: **"Centralization** was the **best and most efficient system**. [Everything] had to be **worked out at the top** and **supervised from above**."

HAYEK

The Austrian economist **Friedrich Hayek** noted, however, that **central planners** only have access to **aggregated statistical information**, and **many decisions can only be handled by the "man on the spot"**.

CHINA

After the **Soviet Union** eventually **imploded**, the mantle of leading **communist** state was taken over by **China**, which takes a **more pragmatic attitude toward central planning**. As former Chinese Communist Party leader **Deng Xiaoping** famously said, "**I don't care if the cat is black or white, so long as it catches mice.**"

THE FALL OF THE BERLIN WALL

A kind of economic experiment was launched on 9 November 1989, when the wall of concrete and barbed wire separating East from West Berlin was officially opened.

SOVIET DISUNION

This decision signified the **demise of Soviet communist rule** in **Eastern Europe**. Former **satellite states** of the **USSR** suddenly had the **freedom to trade** with other countries and **convert to capitalism**. And **Western companies** were **presented with a new market** of almost 400 million people.

THE END OF HISTORY?

The **collapse of the wall** was largely seen at the time as a **vindication of the capitalist approach**, and inspired the political economist **Francis Fukuyama**'s hypothesis that humanity was reaching "the **end point of mankind's ideological evolution** and the **universalization of Western liberal democracy** as the **final form of human government**".

China might have something to say about that – and **Germany's post-war success** is often attributed to its decision to embrace a **third-way "social market economy"** with **strong social provisions**.

ECONOMIC SHOCK

The **fall of the Berlin Wall** led to **massive economic turbulence**, but eventually to **huge advances** in the **standard of living** in countries including **Poland**, **Hungary**, and **Ukraine**. Another country to **benefit** in a **big way** was **Germany**, which – after a **difficult and expensive reunification** – could **exploit its communist connections** to **gain access to East European and Russian markets**.

MIXED ECONOMY

A mixed economy is an economic system that combines both private-sector and government-owned enterprises.

CHOOSE YOUR BLEND

Like **Germany after reunification**, **mixed economies** are typically **characterized by private but regulated markets**, along with **government-directed activity** such as the **provision of pensions**, **healthcare**, and **unemployment benefits**.

The exact blend varies. For example, **Canada** and the **UK** are quite **similar in economic terms to the US**; however, they both feature a (mostly) **public healthcare system**, while the US runs a (mostly) **private system**.

NORDIC MODEL

The so-called **Nordic model** offers a **generous welfare system** and a **high level of public spending**, along with **high taxes**. These countries only get a "**mostly free**" score for **economic freedom**, but do well for **inequality** and **reported happiness levels**. (**Iceland** did briefly experiment with **free market capitalism** in the early 2000s, but it **ended badly** as the **newly deregulated financial sector blew up during the Great Financial Crisis**.)

SOCIALIST ECONOMY

A socialist economy is **broadly defined** as one where the **means of production are collectively owned**; for example, through **cooperatives**. **Socialism** seemed to be **on the way out** after the **fall of the Berlin Wall**, but in **recent years** it has made a **comeback** among voters **even in the US**.

China is described as a **socialist market economy**, which means that **private markets** exist **alongside a system** dominated by **public ownership** and **state-owned enterprises**.

THE IMF AND WORLD BANK

The International Monetary Fund (IMF) and World Bank are known as the Bretton Woods institutions.

BRETTON WOODS CONFERENCE

The **IMF** and **World Bank** were established at a famous **1944 conference** held in **Bretton Woods**, New Hampshire, US, that gathered **representatives from all forty-four Allied nations** in order to determine how the **international monetary and financial order** would be **regulated after the war**. The **key decisions** were **largely made by the Americans**, and to a **lesser extent by the British**, who were **represented by Keynes**.

WASHINGTON CONSENSUS

Along with the **World Trade Organization**, both these bodies have played a major role in shaping the **post-war economic order**. However, they (and particularly the **IMF**) have also seen **controversy** as **critics** accused them of **imposing so-called "Washington consensus" solutions** on **unstable countries** such as **privatization, corporate tax cuts, deregulation, trade liberalization**, and so on, despite signs that the **medicine was not working**.

IMF

The **mandate** of the **IMF** was to **promote international monetary cooperation**; **provide advice** and **other support** to **developing countries**; and also **supply emergency loans to countries** faced with **balance of payment problems** or **debt crises**.

WORLD BANK

The **mandate** of the **International Bank for Reconstruction and Development**, which later became part of the **World Bank group**, was, as the name suggests, to **provide funding for development efforts**, such as building **schools**, **health centres**, and other **public infrastructure**.

PEOPLE IN EXTREME POVERTY – INCLUDING 2030 PROJECTIONS

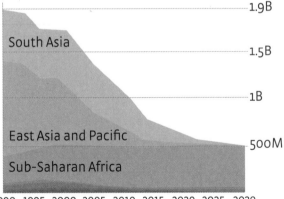

South Asia

East Asia and Pacific

Sub-Saharan Africa

1.9B
1.5B
1B
500M

1990 1995 2000 2005 2010 2015 2020 2025 2030

Since 2013, the **World Bank** has framed its work (uncontroversially) in terms of **"eliminating extreme poverty** by 2030 and **boosting shared prosperity"**.

LABOUR

Labour is the thing that most people have to do in order to make money.

VICTORIAN WORKING CONDITIONS

When **Marx** and **Engels** wrote the ***Communist Manifesto***, it was in large part a response to the **appalling conditions** endured by **Victorian labourers** in cities such as **Manchester**, where **Engels** lived for a spell while working at a **factory co-owned by his father**.

One argument was that **unionization** gives **artificially high salaries** to **union members**, which **harms productivity**. And according to Harvard's **Gregory Mankiw**, "a high minimum wage **forces the wage above the level that balances supply and demand**". In the **US**, the **inflation-adjusted federal minimum wage peaked** in 1968, at around the same time as **union membership** did.

UNION MEMBERSHIP AMONG US WAGE AND SALARY WORKERS

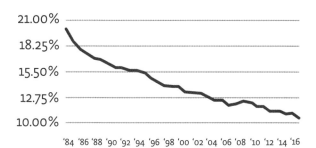

21.00%
18.25%
15.50%
12.75%
10.00%

'84 '86 '88 '90 '92 '94 '96 '98 '00 '02 '04 '06 '08 '10 '12 '14 '16

UNIONS

Working conditions gradually **improved** as **unions** were **legalized** and **workers** gained **bargaining power**. By the early twentieth century a number of **wealthy industrialized countries** had also introduced **legally enforceable minimum wages**. However, this progress went **into reverse** around the 1980s, in part because of the **interventions of economists**.

AI

Today, the **bargaining power of workers** in rich countries has been further eroded by **hyper-globalization**, as well as by the fact that, with **the advent of artificial intelligence and robotics**, they increasingly find themselves **competing against machines**. (Of course, this may change once the machines become **intelligent enough** to ask for rises themselves.)

On the bright side, **many workers in countries such as China** have seen **big improvements in working conditions**.

THE ROLE OF GOVERNMENT

The optimal role of government is often debated in economics.

SHRINK THE STATE

On one hand, **governments** are not subject to the **same competitive forces as private firms**, which means they are often viewed with **suspicion** or worse. **Milton Friedman** once quipped that "If you put the **federal government** in charge of the **Sahara Desert**, in five years there would be a **shortage of sand**."

BASIC NEEDS

On the other hand, even **Friedman** acknowledged that the **state is needed** to "**police the system, establish conditions favourable** to **competition** and **prevent monopoly, provide** a **stable monetary framework**, and **relieve acute misery and distress**".

Many economists agree with the idea that **government should supply things like unemployment insurance, social security**, and **health insurance**, which are not well supplied by **private schemes**. **Public education** also has "**positive externalities**", such as an **educated workforce**. And the role of the government in an emergency was highlighted by the **COVID-19 pandemic**.

INDUSTRIAL POLICY

Some economists believe that the **government** should have a **more active role** in shaping things like **industrial policy**. In the **US** this is **officially frowned upon**, even though **state-sponsored military research and development** is responsible for **key innovations** such as the **internet**, **GPS**, **touchscreens**, and so on.

REGULATION

Preventing monopolies also requires a **strong state**, especially when the monopolies are the world's **most powerful companies**, like **Facebook** and **Google**. When Facebook bought its rivals **Instagram** and **WhatsApp**, it effectively **monopolized** the attention of **billions of people** around the world, which was **not good for competition**.

ECONOMIC MODEL

In economics, a model refers to an abstract, usually mathematical, representation of an economy, which can be used to test ideas or make predictions. Examples range from the "law of supply and demand" to the more complex models used by macroeconomists to simulate the economy as a whole.

STATE YOUR BELIEFS

Since the time of the **first neoclassical economists** such as **Jevons** and **Walras**, economics has become **increasingly mathematical**. A **strength** of **mathematical models** is that they **force economists to state their assumptions** in a **non-ambiguous manner. Model predictions** can also be **checked against real data**.

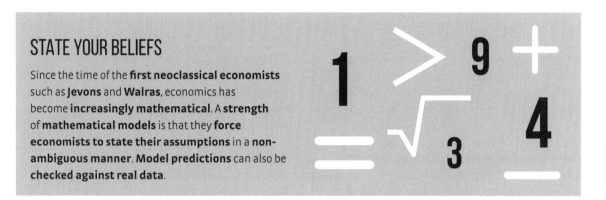

MODEL ABUSE

A **weakness of mathematical models** is that, in practice, the **assumptions** and the **structure of the model** can only be understood by a **small class of like-minded experts**, which makes them **open to abuse**. As discussed later, **mathematical models** played a **key role** in the **Great Financial Crisis**, not just because the models used by **macroeconomists failed to predict the crisis**, but because the ones used by **financiers** and **regulators** alike **helped to cause it**.

USE WITH CARE

Mathematical models must therefore be **used with care**, and the **results** and **assumptions clearly communicated**. As the neoclassical economist **Alfred Marshall** described his method:

1 Use **mathematics** as **shorthand language**, rather than as an **engine of inquiry**.
2 **Keep to them** till you have done.
3 **Translate** into English.
4 Then **illustrate** by **examples** that are important in **real life**.
5 **Burn the mathematics**.
6 If you can't succeed in (4), burn (3). This I do often.

WILLIAM PETTY

One of the first scientists to take a mathematical approach to the economy was William Petty (1623–87), who served as chief medical officer to the army in Ireland, before accepting a post leading an effort to map the whole of Ireland.

MAPPING THE TERRITORY

William Petty's mapping involved **recording the details** of **each parcel of land**, including **ownership**, and **earnings** in **farming** or **rent**. The value of the land was computed at **twenty times the annual income**.

One problem was what to do about pieces of land where **ownership was unknown or contested**. A hint to the solution was that, after the three-year project had ended, Petty was suddenly a **wealthy landowner with estates throughout Ireland**.

MEASURING THE ECONOMY

Returning to England, where he became a **founding member**, along with leading scientists such as **Newton**, of the **Royal Society**, Petty produced the **first detailed measurement of the national economy**, long before the invention of **GDP**.

Petty estimated:
Total population: 6 million people.
Average spending per year: £7 per person.
Total spending: £42 million.

Amount of rentable land: 24 million acres.
Average rent: £0.33 per acre.
Total income from rent: £8 million.

Return on capital investments: £8 million.

THE VALUE OF LABOUR

Since **total income** had to equal **total expenditure**, Petty deduced that **labour** had to be **providing the remaining £26 million of income**. Assuming that land, **labour**, and **capital** all produced the **same return on investment** of 5 per cent, he deduced that the **total value of the labour force** therefore had to be **£520 million**.

LAISSEZ-FAIRE ECONOMICS

François Quesnay (1694–1774) received his university training in medicine. Influenced by William Harvey's earlier discovery of the circulation of blood, he argued that money acted in a similar way, redistributing energy between the three classes of farmers, proprietors, and artisans.

TABLEAU ÉCONOMIQUE

The ultimate source of **energy** in the economy was **agriculture**. **Quesnay's 1758 *Tableau économique*** illustrated the process using an **early version of an economic model** that was based on **quantitative estimates** of the **real French economy**.

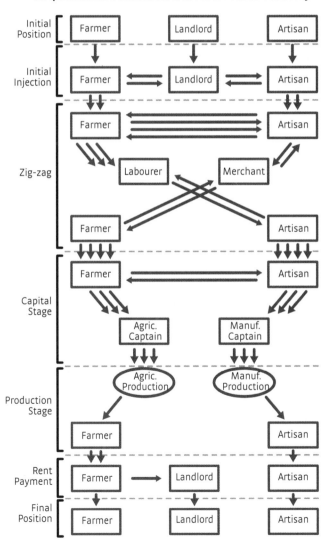

THE PHYSIOCRATS

Quesnay led a group known as the **Physiocrats**, who are considered to be the **first properly organized group of economists**. For the Physiocrats, the **only productive class** that generated a **surplus** was the **farmers**. They argued that since **wealth originated from the land**, the **simplest way** for the state to **raise money** would be a **single tax on landowners**, who **did nothing but collect rent**.

LAISSEZ-FAIRE

The **rest of the economy** should be allowed to **flow unimpeded** – a **philosophy** they described using the term ***laissez-faire*** ("let do"). While the Physiocrats **did not win over many French landowners in pre-revolutionary France**, their laissez-faire approach was influential on economists including **Adam Smith**, and the **Austrian School**.

LÉON WALRAS

The French economist Léon Walras (1834–1910) was one of the founders of neoclassical economics.

ELEMENTS OF ECONOMICS

Working at the **University of Lausanne**, Walras – in his 1874 book *Elements of Pure Economics* – developed the **first mathematical model** of a **market trading multiple goods**.

Adam Smith had argued that **markets find an equilibrium between buyers and sellers**. Walras made this concrete by assuming that **prices start off with an initial value**, then **adjust until buyers and sellers are in agreement**.

STATIC EQUILIBRIUM

Walras represented the process using a **complicated set of mathematical equations**. While he **could not solve the equations himself**, he **could prove that** in principle an **equilibrium solution should exist**.

Walras' model seemed to **put the field of economics onto a more scientific level**, and was a forerunner of the equilibrium models used by economists today.

GROPING YOUR WAY

The process was **complicated** by the fact that, in a **market for multiple goods**, a **change in the price of one good** has **ripple effects on the prices of other goods**. Walras therefore assumed the presence of an **auctioneer**, to whom **buyers** and **sellers** would **submit schedules** detailing **how much they would buy or sell at each price**. The auctioneer would **adjust the prices** in a process of "**groping**" or *tatonnement* until they **converged** on an **equilibrium**, where **supply matched demand** and the **market cleared**.

THE PARETO PRINCIPLE

Vilfredo Pareto was an Italian economist who took over Walras' position as chair of political economy at Lausanne, and whose contributions included the concepts of Pareto efficiency, and the Pareto principle.

PARETO EFFICIENCY

Pareto efficiency refers to **an economy that has achieved a kind of optimal equilibrium**, where **nothing can be changed** without making **at least one person worse off**. The Pareto principle denotes a **highly skewed distribution** where **most of the wealth and power** is **controlled by a small number of people**.

(The fact that these are **not incompatible** suggests one reason why economics has **struggled to address** the **issue of inequality**.)

THE 80/20 RULE

The Pareto principle, also known as the **80/20 rule**, was based on his **observation** that in **Italy** and other countries, **20 per cent of the people held about 80 per cent of the wealth**.

SCALE FREE

Furthermore, **wealth** followed a so-called **scale-free distribution**, which means that there is **no typical degree or average scale of wealth**: **most people have little money**, but **a few are fabulously rich**.

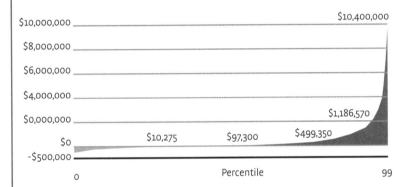

In **business**, it is often said that **20 per cent of the clients** generate **80 per cent of the sales**. In fact this type of **scale-free distribution** is a **signature of complex systems dominated by positive feedback effects** (e.g. "the **rich get richer**"). It also applies to many **natural systems**, such as earthquakes – **most are small** tremors, but there are a **small number of extreme events**.

THE IS–LM MODEL

The IS–LM model, derived by British economist John Hicks in 1937, was an attempt to sum up key aspects of Keynesian economics in a single diagram. It is similar to the supply and demand plot, but instead of price versus quantity it shows interest rate (the price of money) versus output.

INVESTMENTS AND SAVINGS

The **IS curve** shows **points** that **balance investments** and **savings**. This curve **slopes down**, because a **lower interest rate leads to higher investment**, which in turn **increases output**.

LIQUIDITY AND MONEY

The **LM curve** shows **points** that **balance the supply of money** (as determined by a **central bank**) with "liquidity preference" (the **demand for money**). This curve **slopes up**, because **higher output increases income** and the **demand for money**, and therefore **requires a higher interest rate**.

ECONOMIC EQUILIBRIUM

The **intersection of the two curves** represents the **equilibrium point of interest rates** and **output**. The figure can be used to explore the **effects of policy changes**. For example, an **increase in government spending shifts the IS curve to the right** (by an amount factored up by the **multiplier**), thus **raising equilibrium output. Increasing the money supply shifts the LM curve downwards**, so **lowers interest rates**.

The IS–LM model won **Hicks** a **Nobel Prize** and is still **taught in universities**, though he later warned that it relied on a "**drastic use of equilibrium methods**".

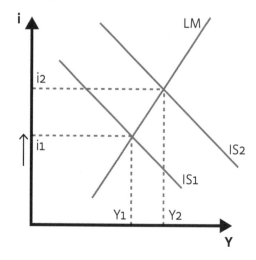

THE PHILLIPS CURVE

Another key component of the neoclassical synthesis was the Phillips curve,
proposed by the New Zealand economist A.W. Phillips (1914–75).

DATA ANALYSIS

In the **classical model**, **inflation** was assumed to have **no significant effects** since what counted was **real prices**, rather than **nominal prices**. However, based on his **statistical analysis** of **British financial data** over nearly a century, **Phillips** argued that there was an **inverse relationship** between **nominal wage changes** and **unemployment**. The **higher the rises**, the **fewer the number of people actually working**.

UNEMPLOYMENT VS INFLATION

The Phillips curve implied that there was a **clear trade-off** between **unemployment** and **inflation**. The **government** could therefore use **Keynesian policy measures** to **stimulate the economy** to reduce unemployment, but **only to an extent where inflation did not run out of control**.

STAGFLATION

The neat relationship between **inflation** and **unemployment** did seem to hold into the **1960s**, but **broke** down in the **1970s**, when it turned out that an economy could enjoy both **high inflation** and **high unemployment** at the **same time** (**stagflation**).

NATURAL RATE

Variants of the Phillips curve are **still used** by **economists**, and in the **financial press**, to discuss **short-term effects**. However, many economists now prefer to think in terms of an **equally controversial notion** known as the **natural rate of unemployment**, which is the (theoretical) **lowest rate of unemployment** at which the **jobs market** can be in **equilibrium**.

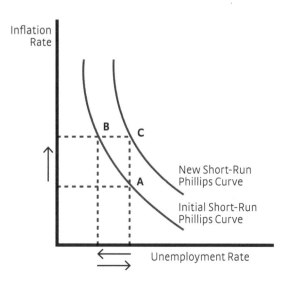

EXPECTED UTILITY THEORY

The mathematician John von Neumann (1903–57) learned about Walras' Elements of Pure Economics and realized that economic transactions could be treated mathematically as a kind of game, in which buyers and sellers each try to optimize their utility

GAME THEORY

In his *Theory of Games and Economic Behaviour*, co-authored with economist **Oskar Morgenstern**, **von Neumann** laid out a theory of **expected utility**, which described how a **rational person** would **make decisions** when the **outcomes are uncertain**.

Such a decision could be viewed as a kind of **lottery** that gives a chance of a particular **pay-out**. The **expected utility** of the lottery is the **utility** of the pay-out, multiplied by the **probability** of the pay-out.

If a person was faced with a **choice between two alternatives**, they would choose the one with the **higher expected utility**. For the theory to be **consistent**, though, it had to make **multiple assumptions**, such as that people have **fixed preferences**.

DIMINISHING MARGINAL UTILITY

The **utility** of a **lottery pay-out** was **not necessarily the same** as the pay-out. This idea goes back to the eighteenth-century mathematician **Daniel Bernoulli**, who suggested that in **psychological terms** the **marginal utility of money flattens out for larger amounts**: a **rich person** gets **less pleasure** from a **little extra cash** than a **poor person** might. **Expected utility theory** was **further modified** by **behavioural psychologists**, as discussed below.

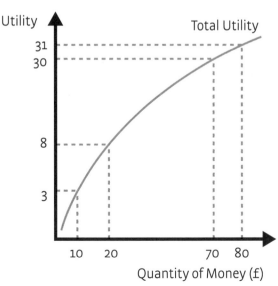

THE PRISONER'S DILEMMA

For von Neumann, the essence of economics was that a person had to think not just about their own actions, but also about those of other people. An example is the problem known as the prisoner's dilemma.

JAIL TIME

This involves two **imaginary criminals** who have been arrested for a crime and held separately. The **prosecutor** offers **each prisoner** a **choice: testify** that **the other person committed the crime**, or **remain silent**. If both prisoners remain silent, they **each get one year** on the **lesser charge**. If **both prisoners betray the other**, they **each get two years**. If **only one prisoner betrays the other**, he **gets off** and the **other gets the full three years**.

Therefore, if a prisoner **chooses to not testify**, the **sentence** is **either one or three years**. If we assume **each is equally likely**, the average **expected sentence is two years**.

If he **chooses to betray**, then his **sentence** is **either zero years or two years**, with an **expected sentence of one year**. The **rational prisoner will therefore choose to betray**.

COLD WAR GAME

The **prisoner's dilemma game** was **first used** in the 1950s to **analyse strategies** in the **Cold War**, and has been used to explain why **cartels** (e.g. OPEC) **have trouble preventing their members from surreptitiously cheating**.

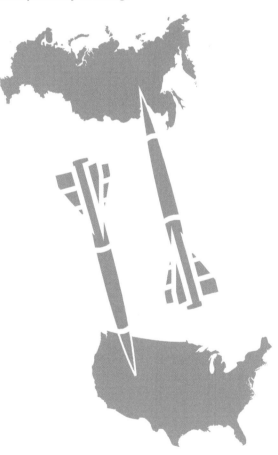

Of course, in a **real prison** a **different kind of game theory** comes into play, where the **outcome for cheats** is generally **less positive**.

THE ARROW–DEBREU MODEL

In the 1950s, the economists Kenneth Arrow and Gérard Debreu developed a detailed model of an idealized market economy, which built on that of Walras.

INVISIBLE HAND THEOREM

Arrow and **Debreu** employed a so-called **fixed-point theorem** from **game theory** to prove that the **market would attain an optimal fixed point**, in which **nothing can be changed without making at least one person worse off** (**Pareto optimality**).

The result was soon being called the "**invisible hand theorem**" because it seemed to provide **mathematical proof of Smith's theory** that **free markets are inherently self-stabilizing** and **set prices to their optimal levels**.

CROWN JEWEL

During the **Cold War**, the Arrow–Debreu model also had useful **propaganda value** in showing that **capitalism**, rather than **communism**, was the **best guide to organizing society**. It soon came to be viewed as the **crown jewel of neoclassical economics**, and inspired the **development of the equilibrium models** that are **still used by policy-makers today**.

HYPER-RATIONALITY

However, the proof of **Arrow and Debreu's model** relied on **extending the powers of rational economic man** so that they included things like **infinite computational power** and the **ability to devise plans for every future eventuality**.

The model also **left out anything that might impede perfect competition**, and represented what amounted to a **barter economy**, having **no role for money**.

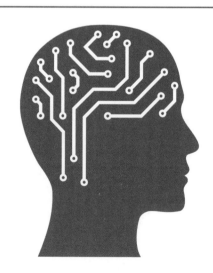

THE REPRESENTATIVE AGENT

Early economists did not have the tools to model individual agents; however, they argued that it was enough to model a single representational agent. The same strategy is often used today.

MICRO-FOUNDATIONS

The idea of a **representative agent** went back to the French scientist **Adolphe Quetelet** (1796–1874), who argued that a society could be analysed in terms of *l'homme moyen*, or the "**average man**".

Many **modern economic models** continue to use **representative agents** to **stand in** for **consumers** or **producers**. For example, an **aggregate demand curve** can be viewed as the **average demand over a society**, or as the **demand of an average person**. The **properties of the whole** are therefore **derived from an analysis of individual behaviour** (what economists call **micro-foundations**).

FALLACY OF COMPOSITION

This leads to **problems**, however, because of the "**fallacy of composition**" – **what is true for a member of a group need not be true for the group as a whole**. It might be **rational for a single person to stand up at a concert for a better view**, but the **benefits** are **negated if everyone stands up**. **Group behaviour** has its **own dynamics**.

NO ONE IS AVERAGE

The use of **representational agents** also means that **models cannot address the details of how markets are organized**, or **issues such as inequality**. Even the concept of an **average person isn't meaningful for things like wealth**, which follows a very **skewed** (scale-free) distribution. In the US, **the average worker earns around $57,000**, but results do vary – **the average CEO earns around 270 times that** amount. Globally, the differences are of course even **starker**. According to Oxfam, **the 22 richest men have more wealth than all the women in Africa**. Inequality is one reason there is a growing trend, as discussed below, to use **agent-based models**, which **represent individuals directly**.

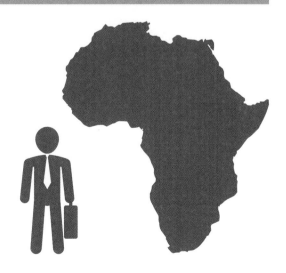

THE DSGE MODEL

DSGE models have been called the workhorse of macroeconomics, and are used by economists to simulate the economy and make policy recommendations.

WHAT IT STANDS FOR

The letters stand for **Dynamic Stochastic General Equilibrium**.

"**Equilibrium**" means that the model assumes, like the older models of **Walras** and **Arrow–Debreu**, that the **economy has a stable equilibrium**.

"**General**" means that the model is supposed to include **all markets**. However, the models are based on a **barter view of the economy** and do not usually include a full (or any) representation of the **financial sector**.

"**Stochastic**" means that the model includes **random perturbations**, such as **commodity price shocks** or **technological developments**, which are treated as **external effects**.

"**Dynamic**" means that the models show how the economy **restores equilibrium after such shocks**.

For example, the figure shows how a number of **economic variables** adjust to a "**preference shock**" at the **start of the simulation**, where **consumers change their behaviour** for some reason.

FRICTION

Following the **2007/8 Financial Crisis**, economists have attempted to **improve DSGE models** by **incorporating various "frictions"** that **inhibit the path to equilibrium**. A **deeper problem**, though, is that the models **assume the existence of an equilibrium in the first place**, which means that they are **ill-equipped to understand effects such as financial instability**.

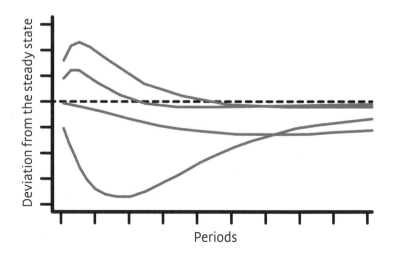

ECONOMETRICS

Econometrics – meaning "economic measurement" – uses statistical methods to analyse the economy

REGRESSION

The main tool of **econometrics** is **regression analysis**, which basically means **fitting a straight line to data**. If **one variable** is **plotted against another**, and the **data seems to follow a straight-line relationship**, then an **econometrician can argue that the two variables are correlated with one another**, and **perhaps linked** through some **causal explanation**.

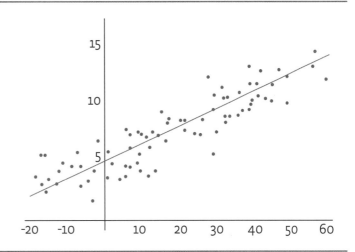

LEGAL ATOMS

As with other modelling approaches, this technique **relies on a number of assumptions**, such as that **correlations** are **stable over time**; that **relationships** are **generally linear**; that **all the relevant economic variables** can be **measured**; and that **everything follows what Keynes called** in a critique "**the atomic character of natural law**. The **system of the material universe** must consist, if this kind of assumption is warranted, of bodies which we may term **legal atoms**, such that each of them exercises its own **separate**, **independent**, and **invariable effect**."

MACHINE LEARNING

Damning with faint praise, **Keynes** said that if "taken with enough grains of salt", the method "won't do much harm". New tools such as **machine learning**, however, **analyse data** with **far less restrictive assumptions** – and in other areas such as **healthcare** can even **do some good**, by helping to **uncover patterns in data**.

THE UNPREDICTABLE ECONOMY

Economic models are often used by economists and policy-makers to make specific predictions about how the economy will evolve or react to changes in policy. Unfortunately, ample empirical evidence shows that economic models have little, if any, predictive power.

NO CRYSTAL BALL

Some **reasons** or **excuses** for our **inability to predict the economy** include the following:

EXTERNAL SHOCKS

Sometimes the problem is blamed on **external events**, such as a **sudden change in oil prices** or a **political disruption**, which **invalidate the model's assumptions** (**predictions** are only valid *ceteris paribus*).

REFLEXIVITY

Others argue that the **economy** is **inherently unpredictable**, because it is very **complicated**, and furthermore is **reflexive**. If the **central bank** predicted that an **economic storm** was approaching, it would **act to prevent it**, thus **invalidating the prediction**.

EFFICIENCY

Eugene Fama's efficient market hypothesis, meanwhile, sees **unpredictability** as a sign of **market efficiency**.

PREDICTING STABILITY

However, such excuses **don't seem to apply** to an event like the **Great Financial Crisis**. As Nobel laureate economists **George Akerlof** and **Robert Shiller** wrote in their 2015 ***Phishing for Phools***: "It is **truly remarkable** that **so few economists foresaw what would happen**."

EXCUSES ARE ALSO IN TENSION WITH THE IMPORTANCE GIVEN TO PREDICTION IN SCIENCE. AS THE PHYSICIST RICHARD FEYNMAN WROTE, "THE TEST OF SCIENCE IS ITS ABILITY TO PREDICT."

The **main problem** with **traditional economic models** is **not that they fail to make accurate predictions of economic storms** – it is that **by treating the economy as an equilibrium system**, they **rule out the possibility of such storms in the first place**. As discussed later, this has motivated the **development of new approaches** that can **account for instability**.

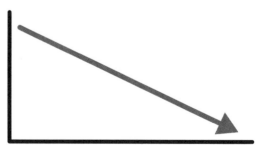

INTEGRATED CLIMATE-ECONOMY MODELS

The Dynamic Integrated Climate-Economy model (DICE) was developed in the early 1990s by Yale economist William Nordhaus, and is used by organizations such as the US Environmental Protection Agency to make predictions and assess environmental policies.

CRISIS, WHAT CRISIS?

In a 2017 paper, **Nordaus** predicted the **effects of climate change** as follows: "Including all factors, the final estimate is that the **damages are 2.1 per cent of global income** at a 3°C warming, and 8.5 per cent of income at a 6°C warming."

While a **decline of 8.5 per cent certainly sounds serious**, it **would take place over many years** so would really represent a **slowing of growth rather than a true crisis** – at least when viewed in narrow economic terms.

NOBEL APPROVED

Nordhaus was awarded the **Nobel** Memorial Prize in economics in 2018 for his work on the project.

However, as forecasters have pointed out, **neither climate models nor economic models are very reliable for making long-term predictions**, and **linking them** together is **unlikely to improve their forecasting accuracy**.

In particular, the notion that **six degrees of warming** is just a **speed-bump for the economy** relies on some fairly **heroic assumptions** about the **economic effects of global climate**

change, and is **contested by** environmentalists. The **Paris Agreement**, for example, aims for a **maximum increase of 1.5 degrees**.

Given that **Nobel-approved models fail to predict economic crises**, we probably **shouldn't rely on them to predict environmental crises** either.

THE HISTORY OF MONEY

Perhaps surprisingly, money as a thing in itself has traditionally played only a small role in economics, but its properties and history can tell us much about the economy.

MESOPOTAMIA

The best-documented ancient **credit system** is that of the **Sumerians** in **Mesopotamia**, whose economy was dominated by the day-to-day running of **temples** and **palaces**. Around 3500 BC, **temple accountants** began to use a **shekel of silver** (about 8.3 grams) as an **accounting device**. The **actual metal** did not **circulate widely**, but was kept in **vaults**.

CUNEIFORMS

Most **market dealings** were done on the basis of **credit**, with **debts** valued in **shekels**, **recorded** on **clay tablet cuneiforms**, and **settled** with **barley** or **other commodities** at **harvest time**. Cuneiforms could also be **traded**, like **endorsed cheques**.

COINS

The **first coins** date from the **seventh century** BC and came from the **kingdom of Lydia**, part of what is now **Turkey**. They were **oval pieces** of a **gold-silver alloy** called **electrum**. These were **large coins** – a **stater** or **shekel** was worth about a **month's salary**.

MILITARY SPENDING

The main **motivation** for the **spread of coin money** in **Ancient Greece** appears to have been the **needs of the military**, which was the **state's largest expense**.

The **state paid the military** in **coins**, while at the same time imposing a **tax** on **conquered populations** that was **payable in coin**. The **only way** for people to **get a hand on** the coins was to **supply the military** with **provisions**.

THE TWO SIDES OF MONEY

Money is fundamentally dualistic in that it represents both an abstract number and an owned thing. These two sides of money are fundamentally incompatible (you can own ten pounds, but you can't own the number ten), which is what gives money its intriguing properties.

CREDIT AND DEBIT

Throughout history, money has **alternated** between **presenting** primarily as **virtual credit**, or as an **owned object**.

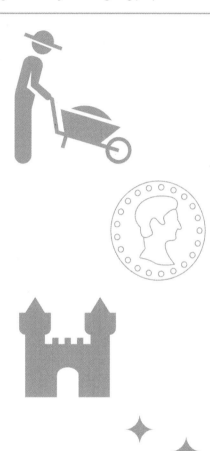

- Early **agrarian empires** were dominated by **virtual credit**, where the **value of a clay tablet** lay in the **inscription**, and not so much in the clay.

- The **Axial Age** (800 BC to AD 600) saw the **widespread adoption** of **physical coinage** made from **precious metals**.

- The **Middle Ages**, which lasted for almost the next thousand years, saw a **swing back toward virtual credit**, with **shortages of precious metal**, and the development of **virtual instruments** such as **cheques**.

- The 1492 Spanish discovery of the "**New World**" with its **massive supplies** of gold and silver saw **money flip back** to its **physical side**, and eventually led to the **establishment of the gold standard**.

- The "**Nixon Shock**" began the era of **fiat virtual currencies** in 1971. Today, we live firmly in the era of **virtual currency**, where we usually **pay** with a **tap of a card** rather than a **piece of metal**.

TALLY STICKS

Shortly after ascending the English throne in 1100, King Henry I – son of William the Conqueror – introduced a virtual payment system based on wooden sticks known as tallies.

WOODEN MONEY

About **ten inches long** and made of **polished hazel** or **willow**, these **tallies** were **notched** and **split lengthwise** down the middle. The **value** was indicated by the **width of the notches,** which varied from "the **thickness** of the **palm of the hand**" for a **thousand pounds**, down to "a **single cut without removing any wood**" for a **penny**.

STOCK OR FOIL

One piece, called the **stock**, was **slightly longer**, and was **kept by the creditor**. The **debtor** was handed the **other half**, called the **stub** or **foil**. When the **debt** was **repaid**, the **two sides** were **matched** and **destroyed**.

At first the tallies were used **primarily** for **tax collection**, but they soon became a **general form of money**. The **stock** represented a **right to collect a debt**, so had a **well-defined value** and could be **traded**, or used to **pay taxes**.

CHINA

A similar **virtual payment system** was used **around the same time** in **China**, with the **difference** that the **tallies** were **made of bamboo**.

The use of tallies in **England** peaked in the **second half of the seventeenth century**, but they were **still in use** into the **nineteenth century**.

GOLD AND SILVER

Gold and its poorer relation silver have long been associated with money. Indeed, one theory of money, known as metallism or bullionism (from the Latin "to melt"), holds that only the metal in a coin is real money.

GOLD MONEY

Money should either consist of **scarce, precious metal**, or at least be **backed by it**. As US banker **J.P. Morgan** put it in 1912, "Money is **gold**, and **nothing else**."

NEWTON

In the early eighteenth century, **English coins** were a **mix** of **low-denomination silver** and **high-denomination gold coins** (a so-called **bimetallic regime**). The **exchange rate** between the two had to be **set exactly right**, because otherwise **undervalued coins** would tend to be **melted down** and **sold as metal**. The problem of **setting the exchange rate** was **entrusted** to none other than the scientist **Isaac Newton**, who was then serving as **Master of the Mint**.

GOLD–SILVER RATIO

The ratio of **gold price to silver price** has historically been in the range of around **12:1** (set in the Roman Empire) or **15:1** (set in 1792 by the US government). However this range **broke down over the past hundred years**, and at the time of writing the ratio is around **100**.

PAPER MONEY

Paper money has been used in China since the eleventh century, and was reported to Europeans by the Venetian explorer Marco Polo after he returned from his travels to China in 1295.

BANK NOTES

People were amazed by **Marco Polo's** description of **sheets of paper**, **signed** and **stamped** with the **royal seal**, that were **accepted as money** "just as well as if they were **coins of pure gold**".

Inspired by this example, **European bankers** and **goldsmiths** began issuing **paper promissory notes** in exchange for **deposits**, that were **payable** to **anyone who had them in their possession**. The notes could therefore be **traded**, rather like the **banknotes of today** (the latter term originates from the fourteenth-century "***nota di banco***").

BANK OF ENGLAND

In 1694 the **Bank of England** was **established** in order to help **fund** the **ongoing war** with **France**, and it soon began **issuing notes** that could be **redeemed for gold**, and **circulated as money**.

JOHN LAW

In **France**, the Scottish economist **John Law** set up a very successful **bank** called the ***Banque Générale*** in 1716, whose notes soon became **all the rage in Paris**. However, the experiment **ended badly**, when a run on the bank crashed the economy. Law, who for a short while was the **richest man in the world**, ended as a **destitute** figure living in **exile in Venice**. As **Voltaire** is **supposed to have remarked** (though **incorrectly** as it turned out): "**Paper money** has now been **restored** to its **intrinsic value**."

FIAT MONEY

Fiat money is so named from the Latin word for "let it be done". Law's banknotes were an example of a fiat currency because, unlike the Bank of England's notes of the time, they were backed not by metal but by the word of the state.

AMERICA

One **admirer** of **Law's scheme** was the American scientist (and printer) **Benjamin Franklin**, who helped **print** some of the **first banknotes** used in the **United States**. The **full adoption** of **fiat money** in **America** was **hindered** however by **English colonialists**, who **preferred money** that was **backed by gold**.

NIXON SHOCK

It was only in **1971** that the **US officially abandoned** the **gold standard** and moved to a **fiat system**. The US at the time was **spending heavily** to pay for the **Cold War**, the **Vietnam War**, and even the **Apollo space program**, and the **dollar** was **losing its lustre** as a **reserve currency**. In 1968, **Milton Friedman** wrote a letter to **Richard Nixon** urging him to **abandon** the **post-war gold-based Bretton Woods system** and let **exchange rates be determined by markets**.

On 15 August 1971, Nixon **unilaterally imposed wage and price controls**, together with an **import surcharge**, and **halted the dollar's direct convertibility to gold** – an event that became known as the "**Nixon shock**". **Other countries soon followed**, with the result that the **modern economy** now **runs on fiat money**.

FRACTIONAL RESERVE BANKING

The idea of fractional reserve banking is that banks act rather like traditional goldsmiths, who would keep a deposit from one customer, but lend it out at interest to other customers.

GOLD RESERVES

This fractional reserve system worked so long as the **deposits weren't all demanded back at the same time.** **Goldsmiths** found that it was **normally sufficient** to keep a **reserve of around 10 or 20 per cent.**

SCALING UP

In the **banking version**, the **state borrows** some **money** from the **central bank**, and **spends it** so the **money enters the economy.** Its **suppliers deposit the money** into their **bank accounts**. Those banks, acting like **medieval goldsmiths**, hang on to 10 per cent (if that is the **reserve requirement**) but **loan out the rest** to its **customers**. Eventually the money is **spent** and **ends up** in **another bank account**, where the process is then **repeated**, and so on. The **net effect** over **many such cycles** is that the **total amount of money circulating** in the **economy** is **scaled up** by a **factor of ten.**

RUN ON THE BANK

Again, this **only works** so long as the **depositors don't all try** to **withdraw their money** at the **same time** – an event known as a **run on the bank.**

While this **fractional reserve picture** is **commonly taught** in **textbooks**, the **modern system** – as seen below – is somewhat **different.**

MONEY

CENTRAL BANKS

A central bank is an institution that manages the monetary system of a country or monetary union.

LENDER OF LAST RESORT

One of the **key roles** of a central bank is to **set short-term interest rates**, which influence the **cost of borrowing money** and therefore **lending activity**. Another is to act as what the financial journalist **Walter Bagehot** (1826–77) called the "**lender of last resort**", responsible for **bailing out smaller banks** if they become the **victim** of **bank runs**.

OLD LADY OF THREADNEEDLE STREET

The **Bank of England** was **founded** in 1694 as the **first independent central bank**, and served as a **template for other central banks** around the world. As the economist **John Kenneth Galbraith** noted, the **Old Lady of Threadneedle Street**, as the bank became known, "is in all respects **to money** as St Peter's is **to the Faith**. And the **reputation** is **deserved**, for most of the **art** as well as much of the **mystery** associated with the **management of money** originated there."

INDEPENDENCE

The **separation of bank and state** is **symbolized** by the historic **quasi-independence** of the **City of London** from the rest of London, and the country. The **Bank of England** was **nationalized** in 1946, but even today the City has its own **lord mayor**, with whom the **ruling monarch** needs to **check in before entering**. Central banks in most **developed countries** are supposed to be **independent from political interference**.

The **US Federal Reserve** was founded in 1913. The **European Central Bank** was founded in 1999 to set **monetary policy** for the **euro area**. The **People's Bank of China** was established in 1948, but is **not independent** from the **Communist Party**.

MONEY CREATION BY BANKS

In most modern economies, the vast majority of money (in the UK, for example, about 97 per cent) is created not by central banks, but by private banks lending money for things like mortgages on houses.

MONEY FROM NOTHING

As **Jon Nicolaisen**, Deputy Governor of the **Bank of Norway**, summed it up in a 2017 speech: "When you **borrow from a bank**, the bank **credits your bank account**. The **deposit** – the money – is **created by the bank** the moment it **issues the loan**. The bank does not **transfer the money** from **someone else's bank account** or from a **vault full of money**. The money lent to you by the bank has been **created by the bank itself – out of nothing**."

REGULATORY REQUIREMENTS

The banks can **loan as much money as they want**, subject only to things like **regulatory** or **self-imposed requirements** on reserves (**money** to **pay back depositors**), **liquidity** (stuff that can be **easily sold** to **cover temporary shocks**), and **capital** (**net worth**, to make sure the bank is **solvent**). In the **UK**, for example, there is **no centrally imposed reserve requirement**. Banks can also **borrow** to **make up any shortfalls**, so **such regulations** are better seen as a **profitability consideration**.

The fact that money is **created in this way** was (bizarrely) **not openly acknowledged** until 2014, when the **Bank of England** admitted that the **textbook fractional reserve picture** was **wrong**.

One consequence is that there are **few limits** on **how much money private banks can create**, which is a **major cause** of **financial instability**.

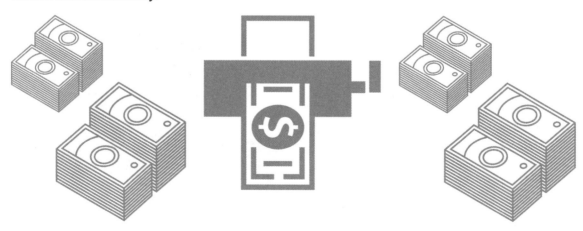

HYPERINFLATION

Hyperinflation is caused by a feedback loop in which a central bank "prints" or creates money to pay off debts, but this extra money has the effect of devaluing the currency.

FEEDBACK LOOP

If the **debts** are in **foreign currencies**, then in **local currency terms** they get **bigger**. The bank responds by **printing more money**, which causes **more inflation**, and so on. People **lose confidence** in the **money** and **trade it** for **other assets**, which further **hastens its decline**. Eventually the **numbers become so big** that the **currency** has to be **redefined**.

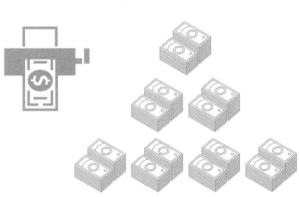

EXAMPLES

There are numerous examples of **hyperinflationary episodes** throughout history. A few are:

- In 1923, when **Germany** went **off the gold standard** in an attempt to pay for **war reparations**, the **inflation rate** hit around **30,000 per cent**. The resulting **economic collapse** paved the way for the **Nazis**.

- In 2009, at the height of **Zimbabwe's hyperinflation**, the *Zimbabwean* newspaper started running **ads made of banknotes**, saying "It's **cheaper to print this on money** than **paper**."

In 2015 the central bank **retired the Zimbabwean dollar**, allowing people to **exchange** the hundred-trillion (100,000,000,000,000) notes for US$0.40.

- In 2018, the **inflation rate** in **Venezuela** reached **1,698,488 per cent**. This meant that **prices** were **doubling** on a roughly **monthly basis**.

The **threat of hyperinflation** is one reason many people continue to call for **hard-currency systems** such as the **gold standard** (or just **invest in such assets themselves**).

DEBT AND DEFICITS

A deficit is the shortfall between what is spent and what is earned.

STOCKS AND FLOWS

Economists refer to the **deficit** as a **flow**, and the **total debt** as a **stock**. If the **government** runs an **annual deficit** then it adds to the **total debt**, just as the flow of water into a tub raises the level of water.

Stocks and flows are often confused; the fact that the deficit is falling on an annual basis does not mean that the total debt is falling – it may just be increasing more slowly.

JAPANESE GOVERNMENT DEBT TO GDP

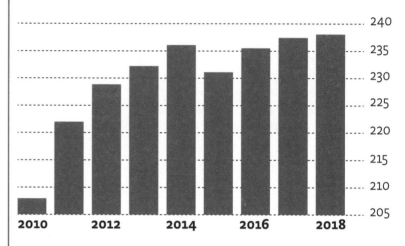

JAPAN

The champion in this area is **Japan**, which has been **running deficits for two decades**, and where the **ratio of government debt to GDP** sits at around **250 per cent**, as opposed to **less than half that** for the **US**. One **advantage** for Japan is that **most of its debt** is **domestic**, while the US is **more reliant** on **foreign creditors** such as **China**.

LOANABLE FUNDS

Classical economists thought about **deficits** in terms of a **market for loanable funds**. If the **government borrowed more money** by issuing **bonds**, then they would be **competing with other people** for the **same funds**, which would have the effect of **raising interest rates**.

However, because banks actually **create new money** when they make **loans**, it follows that the **supply of funds** to be lent is very **flexible**. This is good news for countries running **persistent deficits**.

MONEY

MODERN MONETARY THEORY

Politicians in favour of government cut-backs often like to compare the national economy to a household, and argue that austerity is needed in order to preserve the family budget. As proponents of Modern Monetary Theory (MMT) argue, however, the situation is actually very different, because governments can always make more money.

MONEY IS DEBT

So long as **debts** are in the **national currency**, **governments** should therefore **never need to worry** about **default**. In fact, if there **wasn't a government deficit**, there **wouldn't be any money in circulation** to begin with.

In this view, the main reasons for **taxation** are not to **finance government spending**, but to provide a way to **remove money from the economy** in order to **control inflation**, and more importantly to **motivate citizens** to **use the national currency** in the first place (as opposed to, say, **Bitcoin**).

FUNDING PROGRAMMES

In recent years, **MMT** has become fairly **mainstream**. In the **United States**, for example, it has been suggested as a way to **finance schemes** such as **Medicare for All** or a **Green New Deal**.

Of course, the idea is **not completely new**, but **goes back** to the **invention of money** in **ancient Mesopotamia**, when **temples** made **payments** using **clay tablets**, and no one worried about **running out of clay**.

QUANTITATIVE EASING

If the central bank wants to stimulate the economy, the usual approach is to buy short-term government bonds to drive down inter-bank interest rates. But if rates are already near zero, this no longer works. Enter quantitative easing.

TAKING IT EASY

Quantitative easing (QE) is when a **central bank creates large amounts of new money** and uses it to **purchase government bonds** or other **financial assets** from **banks**.

The name seems confusing (What is being eased? What would non-quantitative easing look like?) and the **results are confusing** too, which is why the **policy remains controversial**.

RADICAL POLICY

The method was **first introduced** in the **early 2000s** in **Japan** as a response to the **bursting** of that country's **real estate bubble**. Following the **Great Financial Crisis**, other central banks including those of the **US**, the **UK**, and **Europe** have experimented with their **own versions**. The **US programme**, which started in late 2008, more than **doubled the Fed's balance sheet** over a space of **six years**.

In theory, the policy leaves **banks** with **more cash**, which they then go out and **lend to customers**. It should also **increase** the **competition for bonds** for a **range of maturities**, leading to **lower interest rates**, which in turn **boosts economic growth** and **raises inflation**.

MIXED RESULTS

In practice, the **results are mixed**. In **Japan**, for example, it has **failed to raise inflation**, and it has similarly **failed to set the European economy alight**. As always, though, it is hard to know **what would have happened** if the policy had **not been adopted**.

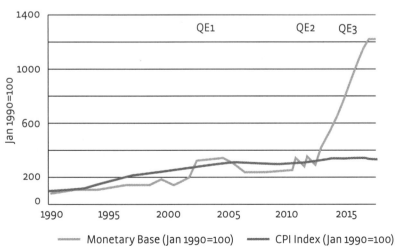

BASIC INCOME

One criticism of quantitative easing is that, by funnelling money into the banking system, it has boosted the price of financial assets, including real estate, which in turn has exacerbated inequality.

QE FOR THE PEOPLE

Some have argued that, instead of making **new money** to **buy government bonds** from **banks** in the hope that this will indirectly **boost economic activity**, a **simpler form of "easing"** would be to **give money directly to people**.

UTOPIAN PROGRAMME

The idea of **paying citizens** an **unconditional basic income** has been around for some time. In 1939 **Keynes** said, "It should certainly have a place in any **utopian political programme**." Indeed, **Thomas More** mentioned it in his 1516 book ***Utopia***. Although it is often presented as **socialist**, the idea also appeals to some **conservatives**, since the government could **avoid micromanaging tax allowances** and **benefits**. Even **Milton Friedman** thought it was a **good idea** (though his version was called **negative taxation**), since he thought it would **shrink the size of government** and **pay for itself**.

SCARCITY MINDSET

While the method has been **tested in a number of countries**, it has **yet to catch on**. Perhaps the **biggest impediment** is **psychological** – our **economic system** is **based** on the ideas of **scarcity** and **competition**, and it seems **morally wrong** to **get something for nothing**. But **much of the wealth** in the economy is generated from things like **natural resources** or **land values**, so it makes sense that **some of the proceeds** be considered a **birthright**. Interest in a basic income has picked up considerably following the **COVID-19 pandemic**.

RATES OF EXCHANGE

Under a floating currency regime, the rates of exchange between currencies are free to fluctuate.

GOLD STANDARD

Under the **international gold standard**, **currencies** were **pegged** to the **price of gold**, except during **emergencies** such as **wars**. At the **Bretton Woods conference**, held in July 1944, the **US dollar** was set as a **reference currency** for the post-war era. **Exchange rates** between **currencies** were **fixed**, and dollars earned through **international trade** could be **redeemed** for **gold bars** at a rate of **$35 per ounce**. That ended with the **Nixon shock** of 1971, as currencies – **starting with the dollar – broke off** from their **tether to gold**.

PURCHASING POWER PARITY

The fact that **exchange rates** are quite **variable** means that economists often use the concept of **purchasing power parity**, which is **similar to a price index** in that it **attempts to measure how much a unit of currency can buy in terms of a typical basket of goods**.

FLOATING CURRENCIES

In theory, this meant that **exchange rates** were **free to adjust** in response to **economic conditions** such as **interest rates**, **money supply**, **growth prospects**, and so on. In reality, such rates are **determined** by the **global currency market**, which is **dominated** by **currency speculation**. Changes in the **value** of **one currency against another** often say more about the **state of this market** than it does about the **economic fundamentals** of the **countries concerned**.

Countries with **floating currencies** therefore **lose a degree of monetary independence**: they can either **set interest rates** to **target a particular exchange rate** in the **currency markets**, or set them to the **level desired** for **domestic reasons**, and let the **exchange rate** go **where it will**.

THE EURO

The idea for a common European currency was first proposed at the League of Nations in 1929, and finally came to fruition on 1 January 1999, when eleven European countries officially adopted the euro.

OPTIMAL CURRENCY AREA

The **euro** is now used by **nineteen** of the **European Union's twenty-eight member states** (at last count), with most of the remainder **intending to adopt the euro in the future**.

One of the **architects of the euro** was the Columbia economist **Robert Mundell**, who was awarded the **economics Nobel** in 1999 for his work on the idea of an "**optimal currency area**". It wasn't obvious that the **European Union** met all the **relevant criteria to qualify**, such as **high labour mobility** and **shared economic drivers**. However, **monetary unification** offered a **number of advantages**, such as **elimination of the need for currency exchange**, a **strengthening of European identity**, and the promise that **shared monetary constraints would impose fiscal discipline on politicians**.

ECB

Monetary policy is set by the **European Central Bank** (ECB), which is unique in that it has **no fiscal branch** and no **powerful central government** to **back it up. Member states** therefore have to **operate fiscal policy**, and **finance deficit spending**, in what amounts to a **foreign currency**. This **tension** was exposed by the **2015 crisis in Greece**, where the country **nearly crashed out** of the **eurozone** over its **unpayable euro-denominated debts**.

CREDIT CARDS

*The invention of credit cards in the 1950s revolutionized the way
we shop, and had a lasting effect on the economy.*

PAYING WITH CARDBOARD

The idea for a **card** with which you could **buy things** came to company founder **Frank McNamara** after he **forgot his wallet** while **dining out** in **New York**. In 1950 he introduced the **Diners Club card**: a piece of cardboard (replaced by **plastic** in 1961) which allowed its **wealthy customers** to **purchase meals** at the **restaurants listed** on the back and **pay up** at the **end of the month**.

PAYING WITH PLASTIC

In the late 1950s, **competition** arrived when **American Express** launched its **charge card**, and the **Bank of America** introduced the **BankAmericard** (renamed as **Visa** in 1977). This last was a **credit card**, which meant the **debt** could be **rolled over** with an **interest charge**.

In the 1960s, **Barclays Bank** in the United Kingdom added its **Barclaycard**, the **City Bank of New York** added the **Everything Card**, later renamed as **MasterCard**, and **American Express** introduced its **gold card**, which was soon **copied** because people always like gold.

THE DEBT PILE

The current **total credit card debt** in the **United States** amounts to more than **$10 trillion**. **Unpaid balances** attract a **high rate of interest**; and the **fees** for **processing the transactions**, which amount to 2 to 3 per cent, are a **major source of profit** not just for the **credit card companies**, but also for a **range of intermediaries** such as **banks**, **payment processors**, and **clearing houses**. The **convenience** of **paying by plastic** means that, for many people, **cash** is becoming something of a **relic**.

CRYPTOCURRENCY

In November 2008, an author going by the male Japanese pseudonym Satoshi Nakamoto posted a paper online that described a new kind of online currency called Bitcoin, which would be "mined" and monitored using computers.

BLOCKCHAIN

"Nakamoto" mined the **first 43,000 bitcoins** himself, and handed some out for **free** to other people he met through **online chat forums**. (Mining is a computationally intensive process for verifying transactions, which rewards the "miner" with bitcoins.)

There had been attempts at **cybercurrencies** before, but the **innovation with Bitcoin** was that **all transactions were recorded** on a **growing database** called the **blockchain**, which was **monitored** by the "**miners**", who **verified transactions**, and **protected** through **cryptography**.

MONEY FROM NOTHING

A year later a **community of users** had developed, and someone set up a **website** that quoted the **price of a bitcoin** as being equal to the **energy needed to mine it** – a task that was made progressively **harder** as **more users joined the network**. At the time, **one bitcoin** was **worth about 0.08 cents**. The price is notoriously **volatile**, but at the time of writing in early 2020 it is about **$8,000**. Anyone who bought $10 worth of bitcoin at the start and held on to them was a **millionaire**.

IS IT MONEY?

Bitcoin has since been joined by a **bewildering variety** of other **cryptocurrencies**, and has provoked much **debate** among economists over **whether it qualifies as money**. In the meantime, though, the people who **bought in early** seem to be enjoying buying stuff with it.

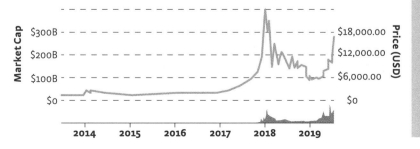

NEOCLASSICAL GROWTH MODEL

Economic growth might be the aim of economics, but economists only started to model it seriously in the 1950s.

ECONOMIC GROWTH

PRODUCTION FUNCTION

The **neoclassical growth model**, which earned **Robert Solow** a **Nobel Prize**, models **output** using a so-called **Cobb–Douglas production function**:

$$Y = A L^\alpha K^{1-\alpha}$$

In this equation, Y represents **production output**, K represents the **contribution of capital** (e.g. **factories**), L represents that of **labour**, and A is a **time-varying number** that represents "**technical change**". The latter was **loosely defined** by **Solow** as "*any kind of shift*" in the **production function**. Thus **slowdowns**, **speedups**, **improvements** in the **education** of the **labour force**, and all sorts of things will appear as '**technical change**.'" The number α is a **parameter** that can be fitted to **data**.

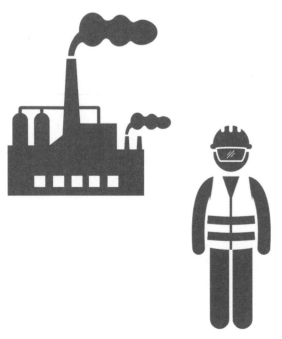

EXTERNAL SHOCK

As a simple example, if **capital's contribution** is assumed to be the **same as labour's**, so K=L, then the **equation reduces** to Y = AL. If A **doesn't change** then **growth simply scales** with the **workforce**. In general, a **property of the model** is that, in the **absence of technical change, per capita growth eventually tapers off to zero** even if **more capital is added**, due to **diminishing returns**. In order to **maintain growth**, the economy must therefore experience **external shocks**, such as **technology improvements**. Because such shocks come from **outside the model**, Solow's theory is an example of an **exogenous growth theory**.

CREATIVE DESTRUCTION

The concept of creative destruction is often associated with the positive effects of unshackled capitalist competition.

INDUSTRIAL MUTATION

The term "creative destruction" was in fact first coined by **Karl Marx**, and its **chief popularizer** – the Austrian economist **Joseph Schumpeter** – saw it as a **symptom** of **capitalism's inherent contradictions** that would eventually lead to its **demise**.

In his 1942 book ***Capitalism, Socialism and Democracy***, Schumpeter describes "the **process of industrial mutation** that incessantly **revolutionizes** the **economic structure** *from within*, incessantly **destroying the old one**, incessantly **creating a new one**. This process of Creative Destruction is the **essential fact about capitalism**."

ENTREPRENEURS

Innovation was driven by **entrepreneurs**, those rare souls responsible for "the doing of **new things** or the doing of things **that are already being done** in a **new way**".

Schumpeter used the example of **nineteenth-century railroad companies** in the **United States**, which **increased productivity** while also **shattering** **established systems of agriculture** by **changing the scale of the market**.

Today, creative destruction is meted out by **companies** such as **Uber** and **Amazon**, and **visionaries** like **Elon Musk**, whose **electric-powered cars** promise to similarly **disrupt transportation** in the current century.

THE BUSINESS CYCLE

While mainstream economic theory is based on the idea that the economy has a long-term equilibrium, the reality seems to be that the economy goes through a manic-depressive pattern of boom followed by bust, with each bust sowing the seeds for a future boom, which paves the way for a bust, and so on.

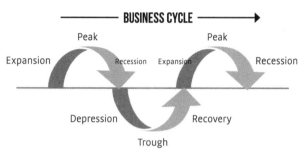

RECESSIONS AND DEPRESSIONS

A **recession** is a period of **temporary economic decline**, usually defined as **two successive quarters** of **declining output**, and often accompanied by **rising unemployment**. A **depression** is like a recession, only **worse**.

THE GLOBAL INVISIBLE HAND

According to **mainstream theory**, **recovery** from such events is a **natural process**, guided by what former Fed chairman **Alan Greenspan** once called "the **global 'invisible hand'**". In the **short term**, after a **negative demand shock**, prices (including **wages**) remain **fixed** but **output decreases** to its **short-term equilibrium**, as firms **scale back** their **inventory**. The **stickier the prices**, the **longer this phase lasts**. In the **long term**, **prices decrease**, but **output** is **restored** to its **original point**, and **long-term equilibrium** is **restored**.

Of course, this **assumes that such equilibria exist** – an assumption that is somewhat **at odds** with the existence of **recessions** and **depressions** in the first place, unless you assume they are **always caused** by "**external shocks**".

SHRINKING ECONOMY

A typical definition of a **depression** would be a **fall in output** that lasts **two years or more**, or alternatively a **total decline exceeding 10 per cent**. The term **first came into popular use** following the **Great Depression** of the **early 1930s**.

The **financial crisis** of **2007/8**, in contrast, is sometimes called the **Great Recession**, which doesn't have quite the same ring to it.

THE VISIBLE HAND

In any case, **governments** can try to **speed** the **healing process** by using the more **visible hand** of **fiscal** or **monetary policy**. The **former** is usually applied to **long-term ends**, while the **latter** is the tool of choice for **short-term fine-tuning**.

HUMAN CAPITAL

Just as the economy employs capital in the forms of machines and infrastructure in order to create value, so people can be said to have a stock of "human capital" in the form of knowledge, skills, creativity, which can be put to economic use.

INVESTING IN PEOPLE

Just as a **country** has **natural resources** that can be **mined** or **harvested**, so **companies** have "**human resources**" in the **form of people**.

Human capital can be improved by **investing** in things like **education**, **training** and **healthcare** (though **measuring the economic impact** is not straightforward).

The concept of **skilled labour** has always been around, but the phrase "**human capital**" was **popularized** by **Nobel laureate** economist **Gary Becker** in his 1964 book of that name. He argued that a person's **output** depends in part on the **rate of return** on their human capital, so **investing in this human capital** will **yield additional output**.

SOCIAL CAPITAL

A related concept is **social capital**, which the US political scientist **Robert Putnam** describes as the **worth of social connections** and **networks**.

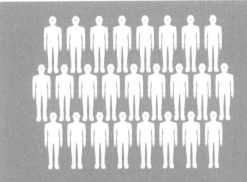

WE ARE NOT MACHINES

One effect of **conflating physical and human capital** is that it **treats people** as if they are **machines**, in a way that would probably have **alarmed** earlier economists such as **Marx**. It also provides an **explanation** (or rather a **justification**) for **inequality**: rich people are **more productive** because they have **more human capital**. This **deflects attention** away from **complex systemic problems** such as **discrimination**.

NEW GROWTH THEORY

New Growth Theory was born in the mid-1980s when a number of economists devised endogenous (the opposite of exogenous) models where growth is internal to the model rather than being imposed from the outside.

HUMAN CAPITAL

Paul Romer, who was later awarded an **economics Nobel** for his work in the area, argued that **growth** is **driven** in large part by **technological innovation**, and **improvements** in **human capital**. Romer was working at the time as a professor at **Stanford University** in Silicon **Valley**, and was influenced by the **emerging digital economy** led by companies such as **Microsoft** and **Apple**.

Critics point out that the **resulting model** is much more **complicated** than the **neoclassical version**, which means that the **parameters** can always be **tuned to fit the data**. As the mathematician **John von Neumann** once quipped, "With **four** parameters I can fit an **elephant**, and with **five** I can make him **wiggle his trunk**."

Also, while it **superficially resembles** the type of model used in **physics**, it **lumps together** many **different concepts** such as **capital**, **labour** (measured by **counts of people**), **human capital**, which depends on **education**, and so on, in a manner that **lacks mathematical consistency** (e.g. in terms of **units of measurement**).

The key **selling point** of the model, though, was that it **offered something the neoclassical model didn't**, which was an **understanding** – or the **promise** – of what **Romer** called "**unbounded growth**", fuelled not by **capital** or **labour**, but by **brain power**.

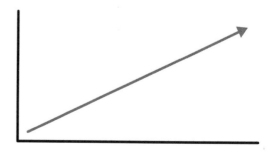

PROMOTING ECONOMIC GROWTH

*While economists seem generally agreed that growth is a good
thing, they are less clear on how it actually works.*

CLASSICAL ECONOMICS

For **Adam Smith**, the **key to growth** was **specialization**, coupled with the **invisible hand**. **Classical economists** such as **Malthus** and **Ricardo** saw growth as the **joint product** of **labour**, **land**, and **capital**, all of which were subject to **diminishing returns**. The **neoclassical economists** formalized this into a **mathematical model**, which included an extra term for **external shocks**.

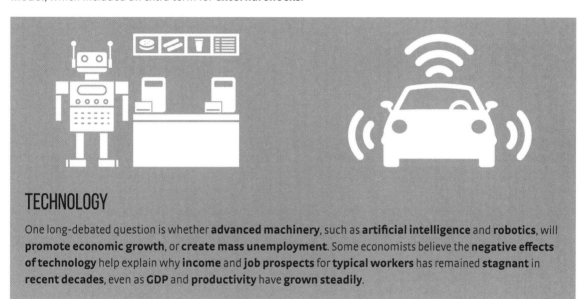

TECHNOLOGY

One long-debated question is whether **advanced machinery**, such as **artificial intelligence** and **robotics**, will **promote economic growth**, or **create mass unemployment**. Some economists believe the **negative effects of technology** help explain why **income** and **job prospects** for **typical workers** has remained **stagnant** in **recent decades**, even as **GDP** and **productivity** have **grown steadily**.

NEW GROWTH THEORY

Romer's New Growth Theory went further by including factors such as **technology** and **human capital**. It also implied that **government policy** has a **critical effect** on the **growth rate**. According to the theory, **open economies** with **free trade** have **higher growth** than **closed economies**, because they are also more **open to innovation**. On the other hand, **high levels of public spending**, **high inflation**, and **political instability** tend to **slow growth**.

While the theory said that **governments should encourage openness**, this **didn't apply** to things like **property rights**, or **patents for intellectual property**. In fact Romer assumed in his model that **innovations** such as **designs** are covered by **"an infinitely-lived patent"**.

SECURITIES

A security is a tradable financial asset such as a bond, a company share, or a financial derivative.

SECURITIZATION

Securitization refers to the process of **turning a future income stream** into an **instrument**, similar to a **bond**, that can then be **traded**. An example is **mortgage-backed securities**, which represent the **income** from **bundles of mortgages**. **David Bowie** famously securitized the **royalties** from his songs into so-called **Bowie bonds** (though this technique doesn't work for most rock bands!).

ADVANTAGES

The advantage for **issuers of such securities** is that they get **access to funds immediately**, instead of having to **wait for the income to arrive**. **Banks** can also use them to get **risky assets off their books**, which allows them to **make more loans**. The advantage for **investors** is that they get access to a **range of investment products** that can help to **diversify** their **holdings**.

INSECURITY

The word **security** is from the Latin **securus**, meaning "**free from care**", but **not everyone who owns them** is free from care. **Low-quality securities** backed by **subprime mortgages** in the **US** helped to kick off the **Great Financial Crisis** when it was realized that the **income streams** weren't as **reliable** as **promised**.

STOCKS

Stocks are a type of financial security – also known as shares or equities – that grant the owner part ownership in a company, and entitle the owner to a fraction of its net earnings, which is paid in the form of dividends. Shareholders also have voting rights over things like the election of the company's board of directors.

STOCK MARKET

The word "**stock**" originally came from the **valuable part** of the **tally stick**. The **first formal stock markets** were established in **seventeenth-century Amsterdam**, and **traded** mostly in **shares** of the **Dutch East India Company** (founded in 1602) and the **Dutch West India Company** (1621).

In the **United States**, the **main stock exchange** has long been the **New York Stock Exchange**, which was **founded in 1792** by **twenty-four brokers**. In 1972, it was **joined** by the **NASDAQ**, which began as an **electronic quoting system** but eventually **evolved** into a **proper exchange**.

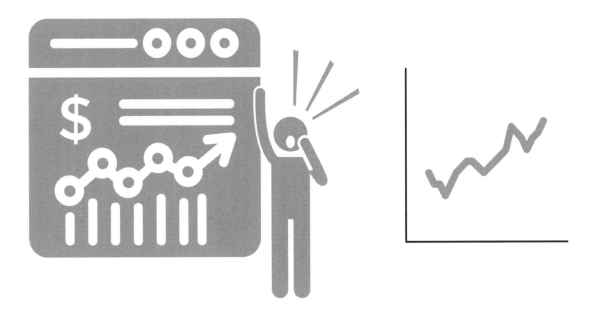

MARKET CAP

The total **market capitalization** of the **world's stock markets** is currently around **$80 trillion**. The **largest** of these markets by far is the **US** at about **34 per cent** of the total, followed by **Japan** and the **UK** (each about **6 per cent**).

MODERN PORTFOLIO THEORY

Modern portfolio theory (MPT) was presented in a 1952 essay by economist Harry Markowitz. Its aim was to determine the optimal portfolio of assets for a particular investor, given their degree of risk tolerance.

RISK AND RETURN

Different **assets** such as **stocks** and **bonds** offer **varying levels** of **risk** and **return**. Bonds are usually **low-risk investments** that also offer **low returns**. Stocks promise **more exciting gains**, but at the **risk of losing it all**.

Investors will often hold a **mix of both**, but the problem of **how to combine a range of assets** into a **portfolio** is complicated by the fact that **assets** are **correlated to a degree** – for example, a **slump in one stock** in a particular industry is often **accompanied by a slump in related stocks**.

EFFICIENT FRONTIER

Markowitz tackled this by assuming that **risk** and **correlation** can be **calculated** by looking at the **market's recent price history**. He arrived at the concept of the "**efficient frontier**", which **defines** the **optimal investment portfolio** for a **given level of risk**.

MPT won Markowitz a **Nobel prize**, and **continues to underpin** the **strategies** used by **investment advisers** (or **robo-advisers**) today. It should be noted though that things like **risk** and **correlation** for a **financial asset** are not **stable quantities** that can be **reduced** to a **single number** – a **problem** that **affects most models** in **quantitative finance**.

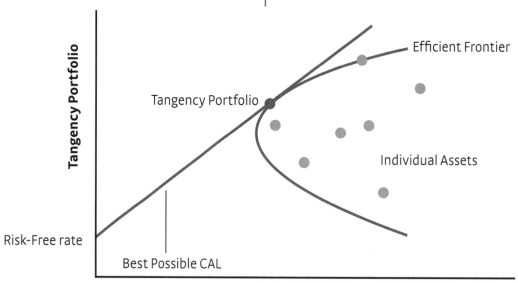

Figure labels: Tangency Portfolio (y-axis), Standard Deviation (x-axis), Efficient Frontier, Tangency Portfolio, Individual Assets, Risk-Free rate, Best Possible CAL

RANDOM WALKS

A persistent idea in economics is that competitive markets drive prices to an equilibrium level that reflects intrinsic value. It follows that price changes are due to external events, such as news about the stock. Since such events are random, prices should perform what the statistician Karl Pearson called a random walk.

THE DRUNKEN WALK

Pearson illustrated the problem in a **1905 paper** with an example of a **drunken man**, who takes a **step in one direction**, then another step in a **different direction**, and so on. The **expected distance travelled** is seen to **grow** with the **square root of time** – but "the **most probable place** to find a drunken man who is at all capable of keeping on his feet is somewhere near his **starting point!**"

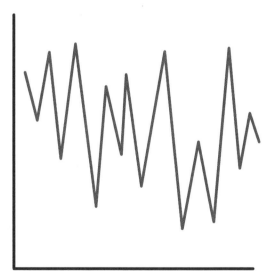

BACHELIER

The same idea had already been used by **Louis Bachelier** in his **1900 dissertation *Theorié de la Spéculation***, to argue that an **investor's expected profit** or **loss** was **zero**. **Prices move randomly up and down**, but the **best forecast** for an **asset's future price** is its **current price**.

OPTIONS

Bachelier used this method to **compute** the **price of options**, which, as discussed below, give the **owner** the **right to buy or sell a security** for a **certain price** on a **future date**.

EFFICIENT MARKET HYPOTHESIS

The efficient market hypothesis was proposed by Eugene Fama in his 1965 doctoral thesis, and stated that efficient markets price assets correctly.

RATIONAL PRICE

Like **Bachelier**, **Fama** believed that **price changes** were best seen as **random perturbations**. However, while Bachelier saw these **fluctuations** as being **caused** in part by **irrational factors**, which **cancelled out symmetrically in the aggregate**, Fama argued that they were a **symptom** of **market rationality**.

THE EFFICIENT MARKET

Fama described **efficient markets** as places where "**competition among the many intelligent participants** leads to a situation where, at any point in time, **actual prices of individual securities already reflect the effects of information** based both on **events that have already occurred** and on events which as of now the **market expects to take place in the future**. In other words, in an efficient market at any point in time the **actual price of a security** will be a **good estimate of its intrinsic value**."

UNBEATABLE

It followed that **markets** were **impossible to predict** or **out-guess**, not because they were **irrational**, but because they **incorporated all available information**: **no one can beat the market**.

Economist **Michael Jensen** claimed in 1978 that "the **efficient market hypothesis** is the **best established fact** in all social sciences" since markets are indeed **hard to predict**.

Critics point out, though, that **unpredictability** isn't usually seen as a **sign of efficiency** (see **snow storms**, **transport systems**, etc.).

OPTIONS

An option is a type of security that grants the owner the right, but not the obligation, to buy or sell an asset for a set exercise price at some specified date in the future.

CALL OR PUT

Call options give the **right to buy**, while **Put options** give the **right to sell**.

If, for example, you believe a **stock will rise in value** over the **next year**, rather than **buying it directly** and **tying up the money**, you could buy a **Call option**. This would allow you to **purchase it next year** at its **old, lower price** and **sell immediately** to **make a profit**.

VALUING OPTIONS

Apart from their **lack of respectability**, a **deeper problem** was that no one knew **how to value them properly**. This only changed in the 1960s with the invention of the **Black–Scholes model**.

GAMBLING ON THE FUTURE

Options are **not a recent invention**. **Aristotle** described how the philosopher **Thales** used **astrology** to predict a **bumper crop** for **olive growers**, so arranged an **option** with local **olive pressers** to **guarantee the use of their presses** at the **usual rate**.

In the **seventeenth century**, options were being **traded** at **stock exchanges** in **financial centres** including **Amsterdam** and **London**; however, they were generally viewed as a form of **speculation** or **gambling**, and **regulators** occasionally attempted to **ban** them. In the **United States**, they came **close to being prohibited** after the **crash** of **1929**, and even in the **1960s** they were only traded in a **small New York market**.

HEDGE FUNDS

A hedge fund is a company that pools funds from investors and puts them into a variety of assets, usually with some kind of clever investment strategy.

BEAT THE MARKET

An **early example** of a **hedging strategy** was developed in the 1960s by mathematician **Ed Thorp** and economist **Sheen Kassouf**. They devised a method for spotting **discrepancies** between the **price of a stock**, and the **price of an option on that stock**. As described in their 1967 book ***Beat the Market***, the discrepancy could be **exploited** using a method that became known as **convertible bond arbitrage**.

HEDGE YOUR BETS

The **investments** are often **leveraged** with **borrowed money**, which makes the **returns potentially higher** but also more **volatile**. For this reason, **hedge funds** are viewed as **alternative investments**, and in most countries **regulators** only allow them to be purchased by **accredited investors** who are **rich enough** to **absorb any potential loss**.

The "**hedge**" term refers to the idea of **purchasing one asset**, while **selling another**, in such a way that the **fund makes money independently** of **whether the market as a whole goes up** or **down**.

RISK MANAGEMENT

Not all hedge funds use **explicit hedging strategies**, but they usually involve **close attention to risk management**. Perhaps the **most successful** hedge firm is **Renaissance Technologies**, whose billionaire founder **Jim Simons** and CEO **Robert Mercer** have become important **scientific philanthropists** (The **Simons Foundation**) and **political donors** (Mercer helped bankroll the 2016 **Trump campaign**).

BLACK–SCHOLES

The Black–Scholes equation is a formula for computing the correct price for an option. It was developed by the University of Chicago's Fischer Black and Myron Scholes, working with MIT's Robert C. Merton.

DYNAMIC HEDGING

The **proof of the formula** is based on the idea of **"dynamic hedging"**. Suppose we have a **Call option** for a **particular stock**. If the **price** of the stock **goes up**, then the **option** also **becomes more valuable**. This suggests that we could construct a **portfolio** where we **constantly buy Call options** and **sell the stock** in such a **ratio** that these **price changes perfectly cancel out**. The result would be a **risk-free portfolio**, whose **return should equal** the **risk-free interest rate**.

RISK REDUCTION

The **Nobel Prize-approved Black–Scholes formula** quickly led to a **massive increase** in the **trading of options**, not only because traders could **quickly establish a price for them**, but also because these instruments were seen, not as **gambling**, but as a **scientific way** to **reduce risk**.

VOLATILITY

A **key parameter** in the Black–Scholes formula is the **asset's volatility**, which is assumed to be a **stable quantity**. The fact that **volatility can suddenly change** complicates the picture, and has contributed to events such as the **stock market crash** of **1987** (**Black Monday**), which has been blamed in part on **failed hedging strategies**; the **1998 collapse** of **Long Term Capital Management**, a **multi-billion-dollar hedge fund** whose board included **Scholes** and **Merton**; and the **Great Financial Crisis** of **2007/8**.

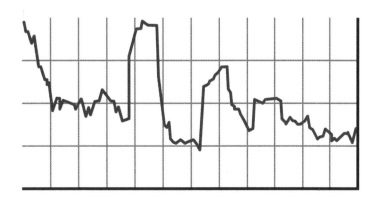

DERIVATIVES

Options are one example of a financial derivative, so named because they derive their value from an underlying asset. In the 1970s, quantitative analysts (or quants) began to apply their skills to a wide variety of more complex derivatives.

EXOTICS

While options can usually be **purchased through exchanges**, so-called **exotic derivatives** are only available **over-the-counter**. An example is an **Up-and-Out Call option**. This is like a **Call option**, but is a bit **cheaper** because if the **stock exceeds some pre-set level**, then the **contract becomes worthless**.

EUROPEAN OR AMERICAN

For example, options with a **specified expiration date** are called **European options** (for historic reasons), and can be handled using **Black–Scholes**. Options that can be **exercised at any time prior to expiration** are called **American options**, and are **much more difficult to value**.

AND MORE...

Derivatives don't just apply to **stocks**; **anything** can be given the **same treatment**. For example, **credit default swaps** pay off in the case of **"credit events"** such as a **company default**. **Weather derivatives** pay off when **certain meteorological conditions are met**, and are useful for **weather-sensitive industries**. **Collateralized debt obligations** are based on **bundles of mortgages**. A **currency swap** involves an **exchange of money**, and the **associated interest**, in **one currency for another**. And so on.

VALUE AT RISK

Following the 1987 Black Monday crash, quantitative analysts realized that they needed a robust method to measure market risk. The method they alighted on was known as "value at risk" or VAR.

BELL CURVE

The **random walk model**, used in theories such as the **efficient market hypothesis**, assumes that **price changes** over a period such as a **week** or **month** follow a so-called **normal** or **bell curve distribution**, which can be determined by **analysing past price data**. This distribution has the shape of a bell, whose **width reflects the volatility of the asset**. A **safe stock** will have **low volatility (narrow bell)** while a **riskier stock** will have **higher volatility (wider bell)**.

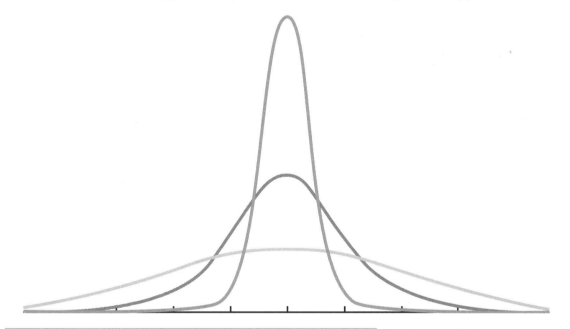

VOLATILITY

VAR uses the **volatility** to **estimate** the **amount** an **asset** or **combination of assets** could **lose** over a certain **specified time frame**. For example, a **risk manager** at a **bank** might use it to say that **ninety-five times out of a hundred**, the **losses** on a **particular portfolio** should be **less than a certain amount**.

As with other techniques such as **modern portfolio theory** and **Black–Scholes**, VAR assumes that the **asset prices** have a **stable volatility** that can be **measured from past statistics** and **used to make predictions** about **future risk**.

THE ART OF RISK

However, as **investment prospectuses often state**, **past performance** is **no guarantee** of **future results**. **Risk management** therefore remains something of **an art as well as a science**.

FINANCIAL SERVICES INDUSTRY

The finance industry provides a range of services including banking, investment funds, credit cards, insurance, accountancy, stockbroking, foreign exchange, and so on.

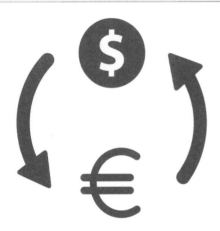

DERIVATIVES

Another major area of **business**, and **source of profits**, is **derivatives**. It has been estimated that the **total nominal value** of the **world's derivatives** (i.e. the **amount potentially at risk**) is around **one quadrillion dollars**, which looks like this:

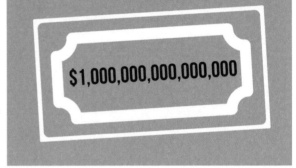

$1,000,000,000,000,000

CURRENCIES

In some respects, the **most important financial activity** is **currency trading**. More than **$5 trillion dollars** is traded in the **foreign exchange markets** every day. For comparison, that is **twenty-five times larger** than the **trading volume** in **global equities**. Most of the trading is **over-the-counter**, conducted through **electronic platforms** rather than **exchanges**.

Most **currency trades** involve the **US dollar**, which is considered the **world reserve currency**, versus a **small number of other currencies**: the **euro**, the **Japanese yen**, the **UK pound**, the **Swiss franc**, and the **Canadian** and **Australian dollars**.

BRAIN DRAIN

While **finance** plays an **important role** in the **world economy**, there can **be too much of a good thing**. A 2015 study from the **Bank for International Settlements** found that "a **fast-growing financial sector** is **detrimental** to **aggregate productivity growth**", in part because it **sucks in talent** from **more productive areas**.

THE GREAT FINANCIAL CRISIS

The financial crisis of 2007/8, also known as the Great Financial Crisis, was followed by the Great Recession, which saw sustained levels of unemployment and financial stress worldwide.

ROLE OF ECONOMICS

As with the **Great Depression**, the **causes** of the crisis are **debated by economists**. However, most agree that **economic models** played a **key role** in **two respects**. The first was that the **models used by banks to manage risk**, and **price complex derivatives**, were based on **flawed assumptions**. The crisis began with a **mortgage crisis** in the **US**, which **spread to other banks around the world** that had **invested in mortgage derivatives**.

The second was that the **DSGE models** used by **policy-makers** were **inadequate**, because they were **explicitly based on the notion that the economy is at equilibrium**, and **ignored** the **banking sector**, which was at the **heart of the crisis**. Not only could they **not predict the crisis**, but they could **not predict the possibility of such a crisis** – or say **what should be done after one has happened**.

BAILOUT

Economists and policy-makers had, however, **learned from the Great Depression** that a **first step** was to **restore** the **health** of the **banking sector**, which they attempted to do through policies such as **bank bailouts** and **quantitative easing**.

POST-CRISIS ECONOMICS

As seen above, economic theories are shaped by their historic context.
Ours is the aftermath of the Great Financial Crisis.

NEW THINKING

In a 2019 speech at the **IMF**, former **Bank of England governor Mervyn King** noted that the **Great Depression** of the **1930s** had sparked **new thinking in economics**. "No one can doubt that we are once more living through a period of **political turmoil**. But there has been **no comparable questioning** of the **basic ideas underpinning economic policy**. That **needs to change**."

Fortunately there are some **alternative ideas** around, which are **not new** but are now gaining **serious attention**.

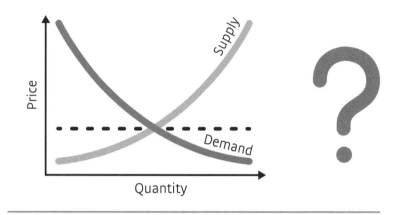

CHALLENGES

Modern economics also has to **grapple** with things like the **AI revolution**, the fact that the (by some measures) **world's largest economy** is now **run by** a **communist state**, **digital feudalism**, the **climate crisis**, the **comeback of mercantilist trade policies**, and so on.

Behavioural economics takes into account **human psychology**.	**Complexity economics** studies "**emergent properties**" that **cannot be reduced** to **simple rules**.

The **neoclassical emphasis** on **rationality** and **stability** led to a massive **blind spot**, which is the **irrational** and **destabilizing role** of **money** and **finance** – a focus of **Austrian economics**, as well as the **new area** of **quantum economics**.

Feminist economics addresses the **key issue** of **gender**, while **ecological economics** sees the economy as just **one part** of a **larger ecosystem**. The crisis has also prompted a **renewed interest** in questions of **ethics** and **fairness**.

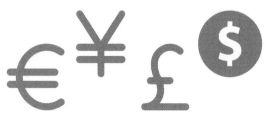

BEHAVIOURAL ECONOMICS

One reaction to the crisis was a renewed interest in behavioural economics, a field that began in the 1970s with the work of the Israeli psychologists Daniel Kahneman and Amos Tversky.

TOO MUCH JAM

Kahneman and **Tversky** performed a number of **experiments**, which showed that people **regularly violate** the **assumptions** of **expected utility theory**. Since economics was **based on the idea** that **people make rational decisions** to **optimize their utility**, this seemed a **radical step**.

For example, **traditional theory** would say that **consumers benefit** from having the **maximum number of choices**. However, as any shopper will attest, we often find **too much choice** to be **overwhelming**. One experiment found that, when **shoppers** at a **grocery store** were offered a **choice of twenty-four jams** to taste, they **ended up buying far less jam** than when they **only had a choice of six**.

JAM TODAY

A more **economically important** example is "**present bias**", which means, for example, that most people prefer to **spend money now** rather than **prepare for retirement**.

Behavioural economics was **initially controversial**, but **won Kahneman** an **economics Nobel** in 2002 (**Tversky had passed away**). The field saw a **surge of interest** after the **Great Financial Crisis**, an event that seemed to offer **conclusive proof** that **markets** were **not completely rational**, and **Nobels** were **also awarded** to behavioural economists **Richard Thaler** and **Robert Shiller**.

COGNITIVE BIASES

The so-called "cognitive biases" uncovered by behavioural psychologists and economists number in the hundreds, but here we look at just a few encountered in economics.

- **Status quo bias**: we **prefer** to **hold on to what we know** rather than **switch to an alternative**, even if it is **better**. This is one reason why **familiar brands** can **charge more for their products**.

- **Loss aversion**: we are roughly **twice as sensitive to losses** as we are to **gains of the same amount**. So, if offered a **gamble** of **winning £15** or **losing £10** on a **coin-toss**, **most** people will **decline**. One consequence is that **investors** tend to **play it safe** and **over-react to losses**.

- **Framing effects**: we **perceive** a **problem** or **opportunity differently** depending on **how it is framed**. Hence the **marketing** and **advertising industries**.

And then there are others, such as the **IKEA effect**, which says that **consumers are happier with a product** when they **have to do some work** to **assemble it** (especially if it is **flat-pack furniture**).

NEUROSCIENCE

Many of these **behavioural patterns** have been **confirmed** and given **physical context** by the **experiments** of **neuroscientists**, who use a variety of **tools** including **brain scans** to **measure our responses** to things like **decisions under uncertainty**.

PROSPECT THEORY

Since many aspects of human behaviour seemed incompatible with the assumptions of expected utility theory, Kahneman and Tversky developed an alternative model, which they published in their 1979 paper "Prospect Theory: An Analysis of Decision under Risk".

VALUE FUNCTION

Key to the theory is the **value function**, which shows the **psychological value** of an **event** as a **function of monetary gains or losses**.

LOSS AVERSION

The plot is **asymmetric** around the **origin** because a **loss** of a certain amount is **felt more keenly** than a **similar gain (loss aversion)**.

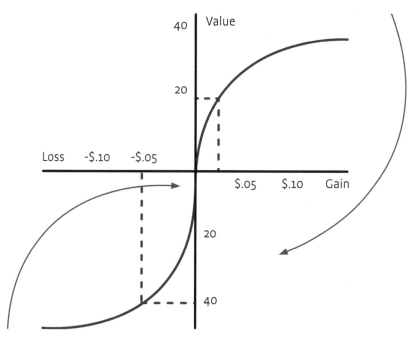

REFERENCE POINT

The **centre** represents the **reference point**, according to which **gains** or **losses** are experienced. So, for example, a **change in pay** might be **measured relative** to a person's **current pay**, or the pay for **similar jobs**.

The **slope** of the **function** is **steeper near the reference point**, and then **tapers off**. This reflects the finding, which goes back to the eighteenth-century mathematician **Daniel Bernoulli**, that the **effect of losses or gains** tends to **saturate at larger amounts**.

UNCERTAINTY WEIGHTS

Another contribution was to show that we **don't weight outcomes exactly by their probabilities**. For example, we are far **more sensitive** to a **change in probability** from **0 per cent** to **10 per cent** – i.e. from "**completely safe**" to a "**small risk**" – than we are to a change from **40** to **50 per cent**. This is why, for example, we **give too much weight** to reports of **low-probability events** like **terrorist attacks** or other unlikely occurrences, though what looks initially like **over-reaction** often turns out to be **the right response for things like pandemics**.

BEHAVIOURAL FINANCE

One criticism of behavioural economics is that it only concerns subtle effects that tend to wash out at large scales and can usually be ignored. However, one place this doesn't hold true is the stock market.

MODELLING THE ECONOMY II

BUBBLE TROUBLE

In his 2013 Nobel lecture, **Robert Shiller** defined a **bubble** as "A situation in which **news of price increases spurs investor enthusiasm** which **spreads by psychological contagion** from person to person, in the process **amplifying stories** that might **justify the price increase** and bringing in a **larger and larger class of investors**, who, **despite doubts** about the **real value of the investment**, are **drawn to it** partly through **envy** of others' successes and partly through a **gambler's excitement**."

According to the **efficient market hypothesis**, bubbles **couldn't exist**, because **assets** were **always priced correctly**. However, the **Great Financial Crisis** had **convinced most people** that they were **definitely a thing**.

PSYCHOLOGICAL CONTAGION

As **Shiller** pointed out, a **major contributor** to **bubbles** is "**psychological contagion**", which **behavioural economists** also refer to as **herd behaviour**. Instead of **making up our own minds** about the **value of a stock**, we just **copy what other people are doing**. The effect is to create a **self-reinforcing feedback loop**, where **rising prices beget rising prices**, and the **same thing in reverse** on the way down.

COMPLEXITY ECONOMICS

The field of complexity economics treats the economy as a complex system with emergent properties that cannot be reduced to simple equations of the sort favoured in traditional economics. Instead, complexity economists use tools developed in physics such as agent-based models and data analysis.

MEASURING COMPLEXITY

An example of **complexity-based data analysis** is the **Harvard Atlas of Economic Complexity project**, led by economist **Ricardo Hausmann**. This analyses the **output of national economies** using "**complexity statistics**" that include **ubiquity, diversity**, and **proximity**.

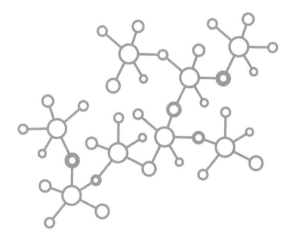

The **ubiquity metric** of a **product** is just the **number of countries that make it**. The **diversity metric** of a **country** is the **number of products that it makes**. The **proximity** of **two products** describes their **mutual similarity**.

The researchers found that **ubiquity** and **diversity** gave **insights** into an economy's **overall complexity**, while the **proximity** of a **product** to others helped to explain a **country's likelihood of developing it**.

DIVERSIFICATION

The project's 2019 report predicted that "Countries that have **diversified their production** into **more complex sectors**, like **Vietnam** and **China**, are those who will experience the **fastest growth** in the **coming decade**." This conclusion is in **stark contrast** with the **classical theory of comparative advantage**, which suggested that countries should **specialize** in whatever they are **best at producing**.

SYSTEMS DYNAMICS

Traditional economic models are based on the idea that the economy has a stable equilibrium; however, this is a very restrictive assumption. A truly dynamic model of the economy can show a range of behaviours, including chaos.

GOODWIN MODEL

A simple example of such a **"systems dynamics" model** was proposed by the American economist **Richard Goodwin** in 1967. This involves **two equations**, which describe the **employment rate** and the **wage share of output**.

PREDATOR–PREY

The two equations are the **economics equivalent** of those used in **biology** to model **interactions** between a **predator** (e.g. foxes) and its **prey** (e.g. rabbits). Here, **wages play the role of the predator**, and **employment is the prey**.

As **employment rises** from a **low level** (like a rabbit population), **wages begin to climb** (foxes), until they become **too high**, at which point **employment declines**, **followed by wages**, and so on in a **repeating cycle**.

CHAOS

As economist **Steve Keen** has shown, the behaviour gets much more **interesting** when effects such as **debt** are **included**. For certain **parameter values** the cycle becomes **chaotic**, with **wild oscillations**.

In **mainstream models**, things like **recessions** are assumed to be caused by **external shocks**, but **systems dynamics** show that **chaos can happen all by itself**.

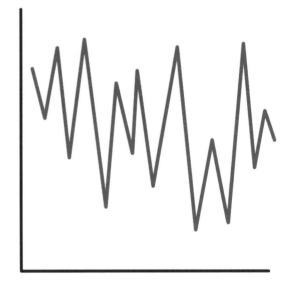

AGENT-BASED MODELS

Agent-based models are becoming increasingly popular in economics as an alternative to traditional approaches. Instead of using single representative agents, these models simulate a population of agents, which could represent consumers, firms, or investors.

LEARNING BEHAVIOUR

For example, an **agent-based model** of a **stock market** would involve **individual investors** who adopt **different strategies** and are allowed to **interact** with one another. Some could be **trend-followers** who **go with the herd**, others could be **value investors** on the **lookout for a deal**. Instead of having access to **perfect information**, they make **decisions** based on **fuzzy heuristics**. They can also **learn** and **adapt** with **time**; so, for example, they could become **more conservative** after a **crash**.

EMERGENT PROPERTIES

These agents therefore **violate** the **basic tenets** of **mainstream theory**, in that they are **not perfectly rational** or **independent**, and they **do not have fixed preferences**, but they are also **more realistic**. The **collective effect** is to **produce emergent properties** that can often be **informative** about the **behaviour of real markets**.

SYSTEMS BIOLOGY

As with **systems dynamics models**, a **drawback** of **agent-based models** is that their **behaviour can be very sensitive** to the **exact choice of parameters**. However, these models have **proved their worth** in areas such as **systems biology**, where assumptions such as **equilibrium** are a **non-starter** (unless the biological system being studied is **dead**).

EVOLUTIONARY ECONOMICS

Economics has always been closely connected with the life sciences. Malthus' studies of population growth were a major influence on Darwin's theory of evolution, which in turn inspired Victorian Social Darwinists and their particularly harsh brand of laissez-faire capitalism.

SURVIVAL OF THE FITTEST

Mainstream economics still tries to "**micro-found**" its theories on the actions of **selfish utility maximizers**; and assumes that **free competition** enforces an economic version of **survival of the fittest**, so **companies that can't compete go out of business** just as **species go extinct**.

ALTRUISM

As biologists **Edward O. Wilson** and **David Sloan Wilson** observed in 2007, though, **evolution** in **nature** acts at the level of **groups** as well as that of **individuals**, and **altruism** plays a role alongside **selfishness**. As they concluded their paper: "**selfishness beats altruism** within **groups. Altruistic groups beat selfish groups**. Everything else is **commentary**." **Evolutionary economists** (including David Sloan Wilson, who also works in this area) argue that the **same applies in economics**.

ADAPTATION

While **mainstream economics** focuses on **equilibrium**, **evolutionary economists** see the economy as a kind of **ecosystem**, which is undergoing a **continuous process** of change and **adaptation**. Evolutionary economists also argue that the **quirks identified by behavioural economists** make more **sense** when viewed from an **evolutionary perspective**. For an **antelope trying to avoid becoming a meal for lions**, something like "**herd behaviour**" or "**loss aversion**" isn't a **cognitive error**, it's a **survival strategy**.

QUANTUM ECONOMICS

Quantum economics is an emerging field that applies tools originally developed in quantum physics to model financial transactions. It combines insights from the areas of quantum finance and quantum cognition.

ECONOMIC ATOMS

Keynes criticized the **reliance of econometrics** on "the **atomic character of natural law**". However, the **real character of atoms** is rather **different**. Far from being "**separate**, **independent**, and **invariable**", as Keynes assumed, they are better described as **entangled** and **indeterminate**. The same can be said of **people** – and the **economy**.

HOW MUCH

The word "**quantum**" is from the Latin for "**how much**", and **quantum finance** is based on the insight that the **answer** to this question is **fundamentally indeterminate** except through an **actual transaction**, which both **acts as a measurement procedure** and **affects the thing being measured**. You might think your **house is worth £430,000**, but if someone **offers £450,000** then **that will be the price**, and people selling **comparable homes** will **adjust their estimates** accordingly.

CONTEXT SENSITIVITY

Quantum cognition argues that the **cognitive effects** explored by **behavioural economists** are best expressed using the **language of quantum mathematics**. For example, **decisions** are **context-dependent**, which is why we **react differently** according to

how a question is framed. This is similar to the **context sensitivity** seen in **physics**, where the **result of a measurement** depends on the **design of the measuring apparatus**.

Quantum economics therefore provides a **consistent mathematical framework** for **studying the economy**, which **avoids the drawbacks** of what Keynes called the **classical "atomic" approach**.

LAND

Mark Twain is credited with saying, "Buy land, they're not making it anymore", and the limited nature of land has made it the subject of much economic debate.

LAND IN ECONOMICS

Economists traditionally saw **land**, **labour**, and **capital** as the **three factors driving economic growth**. While some, such as the **French Physiocrats**, saw land as the **most important** of these, **later economists** increasingly focused on **labour** and **capital**, on the basis that what really **drives the economy** is **human ingenuity**. Nobel laureate **Robert Solow** even claimed in a speech that "The world can, in effect, **get along without natural resources**."

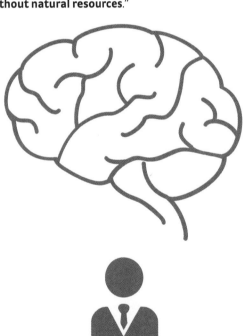

LAND LOCKED

However, **land** has found itself at the **centre** of the **modern economy** in a different way. In a number of countries, including the **UK** and **France**, the majority of **society's wealth** is **locked up** in the **value of urban real estate**, of which the most **important component** is the **price of land**.

In **standard economic theory**, **capital grows** at the **rate of new investment**, and **labour's contribution increases** with the **size of the workforce** and **changes in productivity**. But land is **different** because its **value** – as for an **asset like gold – changes all on its own**, without the need for any **alterations** or **improvements**.

The problem is that, **unlike a gold bar**, land is **basic to human survival** and its **price** impacts on things like the **cost of shelter**. One old idea, that is used to a degree in a number of countries (but not the **UK** or **France**), is to **tax** the **value of land**.

INEQUALITY

The past few decades have seen a reduction in the number of people living in extreme poverty, but also a dramatic increase in wealth inequality in developed countries – a topic that has not been well addressed by economists.

INEQUALITY IN ECONOMICS

Economists have traditionally preferred to focus on **how wealth grows**, rather than on **how it is distributed**. **Classical economists** thought that **inequality** would **lead to more capital accumulation**, which would **speed growth**. **Neoclassical models** were based on a **single representative agent**, so **inequality** was **not an issue**. And for many years the whole topic was considered practically **off-limits**.

As Nobel laureate **Robert Lucas** put it in 2004: "Of the tendencies that are **harmful to sound economics**, the most **seductive**, and in my opinion the most **poisonous**, is to focus on questions of **distribution**." Even today, as economist **Gabriel Zucman** notes, "some people in economics feel that **talking about inequality** is **not what economists should be doing**".

NEW MODELS

One reason for this **lack of interest** is that it **isn't clear how traditional models**, with their **single representative agent**, can be **modified** in order to **take inequality into account**.

In recent years, though, **inequality** has become an **increasingly pressing issue** in many countries, as **wages for most people** have **stagnated** while the **wealth of the rich** has **soared**. At a global level, the **top 1 per cent own 45 per cent** of the **world's wealth**. According to *Forbes*, the **world's ten richest billionaires** together **control $745 billion in wealth**, which is **greater than the GDP** of **most countries**.

Empirical evidence suggests that the **rich consume less**, in **proportion to their total income**, than do the **non-rich**. They also **tend to put their money** into things like **land**, which **boosts house prices** but **does little to stimulate the economy**. A **major challenge in economics** is to properly **account for these effects**, and suggest **workable solutions**.

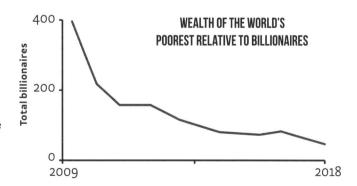

WEALTH OF THE WORLD'S POOREST RELATIVE TO BILLIONAIRES

Total billionaires

400

200

0

2009 — 2018

THOMAS PIKETTY

Thomas Piketty is a French economist who is best known for his 2013 book Capital in the Twenty-First Century, *which – unusually for a book on the dismal science – was an international bestseller, and drew comparisons with Marx's* Das Kapital *for its analysis of capitalism's tendency to concentrate wealth and power in the hands of a few.*

CAPITAL VERSUS GROWTH

Based on his **analysis of economic data** stretching back **250 years**, **Piketty** argued that, in the **absence of events** such as **wars**, the **annual return on investments in capital** (which he denotes by *r* in his book) tends to **exceed** the **annual growth in output** (*g*). This implies that **inherited wealth grows faster than wages**. Therefore **rich families** see their **wealth growth over time**, while **most people** live **day to day** with **no real improvement** in **living standards**.

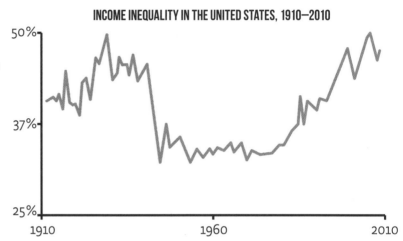

INCOME INEQUALITY IN THE UNITED STATES, 1910–2010

$$r > g$$

If this trend continues, then the **economy will increasingly resemble** that of the **nineteenth century**, where **most of the society's wealth** was **inherited** rather than **earned** (see novels by **Jane Austen**) – as is **60 per cent** of **US wealth today**.

SOLUTIONS

Piketty's **statistical arguments** relied on often-**spotty data**, and the idea that *r > g* is an **iron-clad rule** was **contested by a number of critics**. Even more **controversial**, though, were his **suggested solutions**, which included an **inheritance tax**, and a **global tax on capital – never popular with economists**, who believe that **investment is a good thing** that should be **encouraged** rather than **taxed**.

LIMITS TO GROWTH

The panacea for many economic problems is continued economic growth. However, this creates another problem, which is that the economy collides with natural limits.

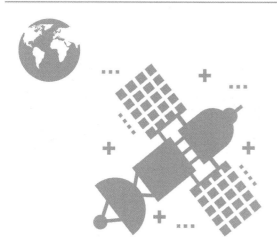

COMPUTER STUDY

In 1968, a computer-based study called **The Limits to Growth** predicted that "If the **present growth trends** in **world population**, **food production**, and **resource depletion** continue **unchanged**, the **limits to growth on this planet** will be **reached** sometime **within the next one hundred years**. The most **probable result** will be a rather **sudden** and **uncontrollable decline** in both **population** and **industrial capacity**."

A half-century later, one of the report's authors, **Dennis Meadows**, updated this with the statement: "**Decline is now inevitable**."

SPACESHIP EARTH

In his 1966 paper **"The Economics of the Coming Spaceship Earth"**, economist **Kenneth Boulding** (1910–93) invited readers to **imagine the earth** as "a **single spaceship**, without **unlimited reserves** of anything, either for **extraction** or **pollution**". Like **astronauts**, he argued, we will have to learn how to **conserve resources**, and carefully **dispose of waste**, which will be something of a **learning process**. As he wrote: "that **fouling of the nest** which has been **typical of man's activity** in the **past** on a **local scale** now seems to be **extending** to the **whole world society**; and one certainly **cannot view with equanimity** the **present rate of pollution** of any of the **natural reservoirs**, whether the **atmosphere**, the **lakes**, or even the **oceans**".

MALTHUSIAN PREDICTIONS

Today, **alarmist claims** about the **environment** are often **dismissed** by noting that such **Malthusian predictions** have **failed to come true in the past**. Clearly, they haven't seen the horror movies that start with a **scientist's warnings being laughed off**.

CLIMATE CHANGE ECONOMICS

Climate change is widely recognized as one of the greatest challenges of our age. Yet, models such as that of Nordhaus aside, economics has so far had surprisingly little to say on the matter. Do we need more climate economics?

ECONOMICS OF CLIMATE CHANGE

Climate change is a matter of **great societal concern**; however, in a 2019 article, the leading climate economists **Andrew Oswald** and **Nicholas Stern** wrote that "We are sorry to say that we think **academic economists** are **letting down the world**. Economics has **contributed disturbingly little** to **discussions about climate change**."

They go on: "**Economic forces** have **largely created** the **carbon dioxide problem**, yet currently our discipline is **hardly visible** ... the **published articles** in our **leading journals** are disturbingly **few and far between**, and **nowhere near commensurate** with the **magnitude of the problem** and the **potential** and **necessary contribution** of **economics**."

DEMATERIALIZATION?

One **oft-debated question** is **whether economic growth only makes climate change worse**, or **can actually help it**. For example, MIT's **Andrew McAfee** observes that the **growth of the US economy** depends **less and less** on the **consumption** of **actual physical stuff** such as **oil**, **timber**, **metal**, and so on. The effect may be **cancelled out**, though, if **consumption grows faster**.

Of course, **assessing environmental impacts** relies on a **detailed knowledge** of the **world biophysical system**. Perhaps rather than having **more articles by economists** about the **environment**, we need **more articles from environmentalists** on **how to manage the economy**.

ALTERNATIVES TO GDP

Implicit in traditional economics is the assumption that economic growth is generally good because it maximizes utility, as measured by GDP. However, critics have long pointed out that GDP growth does not translate into improvements in things like reported happiness levels.

PROBLEMS WITH GDP

In many countries, such as the **US**, reported **happiness levels peaked** some time back in the **1960s**. (This is **despite the invention of anti-depressant drugs**, which are one of the **biggest profit-makers** for **pharmaceutical companies**.)

The emphasis on **maximizing GDP** is also somewhat **at odds** with the aim of **protecting the environment**, as seen for example in the **current debate** about expanding **oil sands operations** in **Western Canada** — what is **good for GDP** is often **bad for the environment**. And **feminist economists** have long pointed out that **GDP omits unpaid labour**, such as **caring for the young and elderly**, which is **often performed by women**.

OTHER METRICS

A number of **alternatives to GDP** have been proposed that **attempt to correct such problems**. For example, the **Genuine Progress Indicator** takes into account things like **social inequality** and **crime rates** (this measure apparently reached its **global peak** back in **1978**).

The **Happy Planet Index** can be viewed as a kind of **efficiency metric** that measures **how much human well-being a country produces per unit of ecological footprint**.

While **GDP** has the appeal of being **based on price data** rather than **subjective comparisons**, these **alternative measures** give a **more balanced picture** of a **country's economic state**.

INSTABILITY

Mainstream economics has long been based on the idea of equilibrium. However, the Great Financial Crisis convinced many that the economy is not an inherently stable system – and that traditional tools are not fit for purpose.

STRAIGHT LINES

The **standard techniques** of **mainstream economics**, such as **supply and demand**, usually involve plotting **straight lines** that **intersect** at a **single point** that represents a **supposedly stable balance** between **opposing forces**.

The emphasis on **stability** made sense in **classical economics** because it allowed economists to **make progress** using the **limited mathematical tools** that were **available at the time**. The fact that it **still persists today** probably has more to do with the appealing (at least to **those in power**) idea that **properly run markets** lead to the **optimal distribution of resources**.

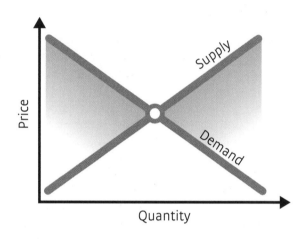

MINSKY MOMENT

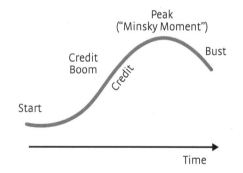

An **alternative viewpoint** was provided by the American economist **Hyman Minsky** (1919–96), whose **Financial Instability Hypothesis** stated that the **credit cycle** is **inherently unstable**: people **borrow more money** during an **expansion**, which **inflates the cost of assets**, which **encourages further borrowing against those assets**, and so on, until at some point – now known as the "**Minsky Moment**" – the **cycle turns** and the **whole thing comes crashing down**.

CREDIT GROWTH

A related issue, as economist **Adair Turner** notes, is that while **banks can create essentially infinite amounts of purchasing power**, assets such as **real estate** are **fixed in supply**. "In economics, when you put together a **highly elastic thing** and a **highly inelastic thing**, you create **extraordinary potential for turbulence**, **volatility**, and for **unstable prices**. Both of those issues are **largely absent** from the way we have **taught economics** over the last 50 years."

HYPER-GLOBALIZATION

Since the 1990s the level of economic integration has morphed into what some economists such as Dani Rodrik call hyper-globalization, which threatens the sovereignty of the nation state.

THE GLOBAL ECONOMY

Globalization is **nothing new**. When **Keynes** wrote in his 1919 book ***The Economic Consequences of the Peace*** that "The **inhabitant of London** could **order by telephone**, sipping his morning tea **in bed**, the **various products of the whole earth** and reasonably **expect their early delivery** upon his doorstep", he wasn't talking about **Amazon Prime**. And even without an **online broker**, the same inhabitant "could at the same moment and by the same means **adventure his wealth** in the **natural resources** and **new enterprises** of **any quarter of the world**, and share, **without exertion** or even **trouble**, in their prospective **fruits** and **advantages**".

GROWTH FACTORS

However, globalization switched into **hyper-drive** due to a number of factors. These include **technological advances** such as **containerized freight** and **improvements in communications**; **political changes**, in particular **China's transition** to an **export-focused market economy**; the **growing power** of **multinational companies**, who **lobby** against anything that **impedes their ability** to **dominate the global stage**, such as **tariffs** or **regulations**; and a **massive increase** in **financial integration**.

While globalization was long seen as a way to **promote economic growth**, in recent years there has been a realization that this **growth comes with a side order** of **inequality**, **instability**, and **carbon footprint**. And following the **COVID-19 pandemic**, many countries see the merit of **producing their own essentials** such as medical supplies.

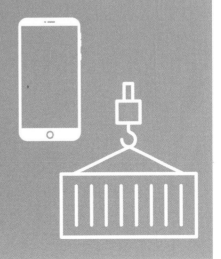

POWER

When neoclassical economists first started to mathematicize their subject, they made the symmetry assumption that individual agents, be they consumers or producers, have roughly equal power.

SYMMETRY

This **symmetry assumption** persists in the ideas of **perfect competition**, where **markets** are treated as a **level playing field**, and the **efficient market hypothesis**, where it is assumed that **all investors have access to perfect information**. Discussions of **power** therefore tend to be **limited** to **obvious issues** like **preventing monopolies**.

However, power affects **every aspect** of the economy, including **wage bargaining**, **advertising**, **legal power**, the **ability to avoid taxes**, the **terms of trade agreements**, and **influence over the political process**.

THE CROWBAR OF POWER

Perhaps the most obvious **power-asymmetry** is that caused by **money**, which **Friedrich Nietzsche** described as "the **crowbar of power**". According to an **Oxfam report**, "over **half the world's billionaires** either **inherited their wealth** or accumulated it through **industries which are prone to corruption and cronyism**". In countries such as the **UK** and **US**, much of the wealth comes from the **financial sector**, which itself holds a **crowbar-like power** over the **rest of the economy**.

Economists are **increasingly turning their attention** to theories from areas such as **development economics**, **evolutionary economics**, and **feminist economics**, which emphasize the **role of power** in **relations between individuals and groups**.

GENDER

Feminist economists have long argued that economics need to pay more attention to the issue of gender – with the starting point being the profession itself.

SLOW DEVELOPERS

In 1973, the economist **Marina Whitman** testified to a **US Congress committee** that "The **economics profession** has been **slow in developing expertise** on the **special problems** of **women**." She was reacting to **Paul Samuelson's bestselling textbook *Economics***, which **mocked** a **fringe argument** as the work of "a **few women** and **soapbox orators**, who are **longer on intuition than brains**".

Things have **progressed** since then – but **not by much**.

SEX DISCRIMINATION

In 2014, when the ***Economist*** magazine chose the **twenty-five most influential economists, zero were women**. Of the **eighty-one people** to have been **awarded the Nobel Memorial Prizes in Economic Sciences** in its fifty-plus years of existence, **two went to women**, only **one** of which (for the 2019 award) was an **actual economist**.

And when the **American Economic Association** polled its members in 2019 about the **state of economics, 40 per cent of men**, but a mere **20 per cent of women**, said they **agreed** or **strongly agreed** with the **statement** "I am **satisfied with the overall climate** within the field of economics."

During a 2019 **panel discussion** on **gender issues, Janet Yellen** said that addressing the issue of **sex discrimination** "should be the **highest priority**" for **economists**. It will be interesting to see **how economics changes as a profession** now that it is finally **losing its aura** as a **club for men**.

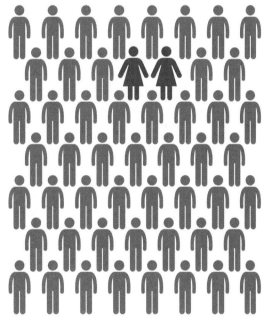

TAX EVASION

According to economic theory, one function of tax is to redistribute some income from the wealthy to the rest. In practice, as the leak of financial documents known as the Panama Papers highlighted in 2016, the richest people and corporations often pay very little tax, thanks to the existence of tax shelters.

TAX HAVENS

About a **tenth** of the **world's wealth** is estimated to be held in **offshore tax havens**. A **third** to a **half** of "**foreign direct investment**" turns out on **closer inspection** to be **not long-term investments** in the "**real economy**" but rather **payments** through **offshore shell companies** set up to **avoid tax**. In **prime cities** such as **London** or **Vancouver**, many **luxury properties** are **owned through holding companies**. The "**Vancouver model**" of **money laundering**, which involves using **casinos** and **high-end real estate** to **conceal criminal proceeds**, has contributed to a **growing homelessness crisis** in the city.

FAILURE TO DECLARE

Multinational corporations make their money in countries with relatively **high tax burdens**, but **declare their profits** in **low-tax countries** such as **Bermuda**, the **British Caribbean**, **Ireland**, or **Luxembourg**.

A 2015 study by the **IMF** concluded that such ruses **reduced annual revenue** in **OECD countries** by an **amount equivalent to about 1 per cent of GDP**.

One **solution**, proposed by the French economist **Gabriel Zucman**, is to **tax the profits of multinational** according to **where they actually make their sales**.

ETHICS

In the medieval period, discussion of "the economy" focused on ethical questions, such as the notion of a just price.

ETHICS IN ECONOMICS

The historical emphasis on **free markets**, and the idea that **market forces set prices correctly**, meant that the **medieval interest in ethics atrophied**, to the point where – as Czech economist **Tomáš Sedláček** noted in his 2011 ***Economics of Good and Evil*** – "it is **almost heretical** to even **talk about it**".

INSIDE JOB

As documented by the Oscar-winning documentary film ***Inside Job***, things started to change following the **Great Financial Crisis**, which brought into **public view** the **ethical failings** not just of **financial traders**, but of the **academic economists** who acted as their **cheerleaders**.

As a simple example, from 2008 to 2010 a stream of **academics** was called to **testify** to **House** and **Senate committees** in the **US** in order to help debate **how financial regulation should be updated** in order to **incorporate the lessons from the crisis**. A study from **Reuters** found many cases where **economists listed their academic affiliations**, but did not mention that they **also consulted for companies** that would be **affected by the regulation under discussion**.

A 2012 study in the ***Cambridge Journal of Economics*** observed that "Perhaps **these connections** helped explain why **few mainstream economists warned about the oncoming financial crisis**."

UNETHICAL MARKETS

Coupled with this **ethical blindness**, is a blindness to the idea that **markets** are **not inherently ethical**. As **James K. Galbraith** testified to the **US Senate** in 2010, "Economists have **soft-pedaled** the role of **fraud** in **every crisis** they examined." Economists need to learn the **importance of ethics**, and of **crime**. **Ancient economics** might be a **good place to start**.

GLOSSARY

aggregate: (noun) a whole formed by adding a number of separate elements

blockchain: a record of cryptocurrency transactions that is maintained across a number of computers, and is resistant to modification of the data

capital: money or assets that can be invested or used for financial gain

capitalism: a system in which trade and industry are controlled by private owners rather than by the state

chaotic system: a system whose future evolution depends strongly on the exact initial condition (starting point)

closed economy: an economy that does not trade externally, so can be considered as isolated

commodity: a good such as copper that is largely fungible, in the sense that it doesn't matter who produced it

complex system: a system such as the Earth's atmosphere, a living cell, or the human economy, that is composed of many interacting components, and shows emergent properties

correlation: a relationship between two sets of randomly varying data – a strong correlation implies that the two tend to vary together, while no correlation means that they are completely independent

crowding out: usually refers to cases when the government is so strongly involved in some part of the economy that it leaves no room for the private sector

default: failure to repay a loan

discount rate: this can refer to the minimum interest rate charged by a central bank for lending to other banks, or it can mean the rate of return used to determine the present value of future cash flows

economies of scale: the proportionate cost advantages gained by an increased scale of operation

emergent property: a property or behaviour of a complex system that arises from basic laws or principles, but cannot be predicted from them

factors of production: in classical economics these referred to land, labour, and capital

Federal Reserve system: the central banking system of the United States of America, founded in 1913

feedback: a situation in which a portion of a signal is fed back into the source, thus modifying the signal, as when a microphone is pointed at a speaker

financial bubble: when asset prices are driven to excessive heights by contagious excitement about future values

game theory: a branch of mathematics that studies strategic interaction among decision-makers

general equilibrium: an imagined state of the economy in which prices are stable and all markets clear

Green New Deal: a proposed package of United States legislation that aims to tackle climate change and inequality

infrastructure: the basic physical and organizational systems needed for the operation of a society or enterprise, such as buildings, roads, sewage, power supplies, and so on

intellectual property: a type of property, such as an invention or a design, that is an intangible product of the human intellect, and that can be protected by copyrights, patents, trademarks, and trade secrets

land tax: a tax on ownership of a piece of land that is usually based on its estimated value

lender of last resort: the role held by central banks, in which they offer support to private banks that are otherwise unable to obtain sufficient liquid assets

liquidity: the availability of assets that can be easily sold at short notice

marginal: associated with a small change to some quantity, as opposed to the total amount

monetarism: a school of thought that says the economy is best managed through control of the money supply

money supply: the total amount of money in a country, usually defined as the currency in circulation plus the amount in demand deposits, though broader measures are also used

multiplier: a factor of proportionality that measures how much one economic variable such as GDP changes in response to a change in another variable such as government spending

neoclassical economics: a school of economics based on the concepts of individualism, rationality, and equilibrium

Nobel Prize for Economics: refers to the Sveriges Riksbank Prize in Economic Sciences in Memory of Alfred Nobel, which was created in 1969, seven decades after Alfred Nobel's death, by the Bank of Sweden

nominal price: the price of a good in terms of money

nonlinear equation: an equation that, when plotted, does not describe a straight line

opportunity cost: the potential gain one loses from other alternatives when one alternative is chosen

Physiocrats: an eighteenth-century group of French economists who believed that agriculture was the ultimate source of all wealth

real price: the price of a good adjusted for general levels of inflation or deflation

reserve currency: a currency that is held by central banks around the world as a major part of their foreign exchange reserves

reserves: money that is held by banks to pay back depositors

risk management: the practice of identifying, analysing, and protecting against potential future financial risks

risk-free rate: the interest rate an investor would expect from a risk-free investment such as Treasury bills

tax haven: a country or place offering very low rates of taxation, and also often financial secrecy, to foreign investors

Treasury bills: in the United States, these are zero-coupon bonds that mature in a year or less and pay no interest

usury: lending money at an exorbitant interest rate

utility: usually refers to the amount of happiness or satisfaction that a person receives from an economic transaction

volatility: a statistical measure of the dispersion of returns for a particular security

zero-sum game: a situation in which one person's gain is exactly balanced by the losses of the other participants

FURTHER READING

George A. Akerlof and Robert J. Shiller, *Phishing for Phools: The Economics of Manipulation and Deception*

Catherine Eagleton and Jonathan Williams, *Money: A History*

Joe Earle, Cahal Moran, and Zach Ward-Perkins, *The Econocracy: The Perils of Leaving Economics to the Experts*

Norbert Häring and Niall Douglas, *Economists and the Powerful*

Daniel Kahneman, *Thinking, Fast and Slow*

Satoshi Nakamoto, "Bitcoin: A Peer-to-Peer Electronic Cash System", https://bitcoin.org/bitcoin.pdf

David Orrell, *Economyths: 11 Ways Economics Gets It Wrong*

Thomas Piketty, *Capital in the Twenty-First Century*

Kate Raworth, *Doughnut Economics: Seven Ways to Think Like a 21st-Century Economist*

Tomáš Sedláček, *Economics of Good and Evil: The Quest for Economic Meaning from Gilgamesh to Wall Street*

Jack Weatherford, *The History of Money*